DIFFICULT MOTHERS

ALSO BY TERRI APTER

What Do You Want from Me?

*The Sister Knot: Why We Fight, Why We're Jealous, and
Why We'll Love Each Other No Matter What*

*You Don't Really Know Me: Why Mothers and
Daughters Fight and How Both Can Win*

*The Confident Child:
Raising Children to Believe in Themselves*

*Secret Paths:
Women in the New Midlife*

*Best Friends: The Perils and Pleasures of
Girls' and Women's Friendships* (coauthor, Ruthellen Josselson)

*Altered Loves:
Mothers and Daughters During Adolescence*

*Working Women Don't Have Wives:
Professional Success in the 1990s*

*The Myth of Maturity:
What Teenagers Need from Parents to Become Adults*

DIFFICULT MOTHERS

UNDERSTANDING AND
OVERCOMING THEIR POWER

Terri Apter

W. W. NORTON & COMPANY   NEW YORK • LONDON

For information about permission to reproduce selections from this
book, write to Permissions, W. W. Norton & Company, Inc.,
500 Fifth Avenue, New York, NY 10110

For information about special discounts for bulk purchases, please
contact W. W. Norton Special Sales at specialsales@wwnorton.com
or 800-233-4830

Manufacturing by RR Donnelley, Harrisonburg
Book design by Brooke Koven
Production manager: Devon Zahn

Library of Congress Cataloging-in-Publication Data

Apter, T. E.
    Difficult mothers : understanding and overcoming their power /
    Terri Apter. — 1st ed.
        p. cm.
    Includes bibliographical references and index.
    ISBN 978-0-393-08102-2 (hbk.)
1. Mother and child. 2. Mothers—Psychology. 3. Control
(Psychology) 4. Families—Psychological aspects. I. Title.
    BF723.M55A68 2012
    155.9'24—dc23
                                                              2011048262

W. W. Norton & Company, Inc.
500 Fifth Avenue, New York, N.Y. 10110
www.wwnorton.com

W. W. Norton & Company Ltd.
Castle House, 75/76 Wells Street, London W1T 3QT

1 2 3 4 5 6 7 8 9 0

Contents

Introduction   vii

CHAPTER ONE
Difficult Mothers: Common Patterns   1

CHAPTER TWO
The Science Behind a Mother's Power   23

CHAPTER THREE
The Angry Mother   43

CHAPTER FOUR
The Controlling Mother   75

CHAPTER FIVE
The Narcissistic Mother   93

CHAPTER SIX

The Envious Mother   115

CHAPTER SEVEN

The Emotionally Unavailable Mother   133

CHAPTER EIGHT

Am I a Difficult Mother?   161

CHAPTER NINE

Resilience: Overcoming a Difficult Mother's Power   187

Notes   207

Bibliography   217

Acknowledgments   227

Index   229

Introduction

IT COMES without warning. I turn my gaze out my office window, anticipating one of those exquisitely private moments when memories and long-term musings sweep away the deliberations of the day. Instead, I suddenly chill to memories of my mother's angry breath and feel its rhythm in my own heartbeat. My enjoyment of the glowing college gardens and the unexpected peacefulness in my workday afternoon is broken by a sudden storm of accusation and derision. My mother has been dead for many years, and in that time I have come to cherish a family of my own and face largely pleasant professional challenges in my adult life, but her critical, suspicious, probing presence is a constant companion.

I count myself not merely a survivor but also someone who has had some benefit from the puzzles and paradoxes of that difficult relationship. In the course of my research for this book, I learned that many people develop skills such as tolerance, diplomacy, compassion, and patience from a difficult relationship with their mother; but for many, too, the impact is devastating. They persist in seeing themselves as the child who could not secure comfort with the most important person in their life. Love, attachment, and closeness are packed with the dangers of constraint, humiliation, and despair. While these past experiences may contain the gold of creativity and may provide a source of energy, imagination, and intelligence, they leave us perplexed, angry, and uncertain. This book offers a framework for understanding what sometimes goes wrong in one of the most formative relationships of our lives and why the effects of this difficulty linger. Psychological science shows why our past difficulties continue to shape our present lives. This science also offers tools to reshape our responses and maintain our resilience.

DIFFICULT MOTHERS GREW out of an article I wrote for *Psychology Today* in which I outlined common patterns of the uncommon experience of a difficult mother. The responses that flooded in by letter and email stunned me. I thought I was describing a few outlying cases, but I soon realized the theme had a wide resonance. Men and women in their teens, in early adulthood, in middle age, and in their senior years said they could now begin to understand their difficult relationships. They expressed relief that it was not "just them" and that the fault was not "all theirs." They felt liberated from an ancient shame. For me, too, there was relief and pleasure in having finally written on a subject that has engaged my thought and attention for many years, but which I had supposed was of limited interest, a matter of rare exception only.

Not all the responses were positive. A longtime friend and valued colleague said that though she found the article useful in her clinical practice, she was wary of the subject.

"Talking about difficult mothers is dangerous," she explained. "Everyone blames mothers for everything. If you focus on difficult mothers, you ignore a mother's perspective."

Anyone approaching the heated topic of difficult mothers would be wise to heed my brilliant colleague's warning. "Difficult mothers" *is* a dangerous topic. First, it threatens to disturb the ideal of "mother love" that is the foundation of parenting models in psychology, in society, and in politics. Common sayings trip off the tongue to waylay the unease so often felt when confronting this topic: "You only have one mother." "She does her best." "You know she loves you." These words bury the uneasy subject. The message is: "You should concentrate on what is good in this relationship" and "You cannot publicly challenge the maternal ideal." In other words, it is better to comply with the relational dilemma imposed by a difficult mother than to articulate the paradoxical feelings that plague you. To this charge, I argue that the cultural pressure to deny complex and unpleasant thoughts and emotions should be resisted. This resistance is a fundamental task not only of the psychologist but of every person who wants to feel whole.

The second objection is that any mention of difficult mothers can be perceived as an attempt to denigrate all mothers. This objection is really a mirror image of the first. Whatever is idealized is always at risk of being denigrated or demonized. When mothers are idealized, the real mother is at risk of appearing to be a "bad mother." The ideal mother is always patient, loving, and responsive. She is perfectly attuned to the needs of others and indifferent to her own. Does "difficult mother" refer to a mother who simply does not meet an unrealistic ideal?

The answer is no. I emphasize the importance of maternal responsiveness, both in infancy and throughout a person's development, but sufficient responsiveness is very different from perfect responsiveness. After all, children have evolved to thrive with a parent who has a normal range of rough edges, limitations, and imperfections. Instead of "good" versus "bad" mother, I use the term "good-enough" mother. In fact, a child needs to experience the quirks, the individuality, and the "selfish" needs of a mother. A child would find the "perfect" mother "too good"; a "perfect" mother would be unable to provide the rough and ready experiences of loving and being loved by a person with her own needs and interests, whose attention shifts and sometimes fades, whose moods fluctuate, whose emotions have their own character and rhythm. A good-enough mother is necessarily *not* a perfect mother, and she reveals her diverse humanity to her child.

The third reason "difficult mother" is a dangerous topic is that it seems to objectively justify a son's or daughter's criticism. Clinical psychologists often hear complaints about a mother and build up, consistently and over a long period of time, a picture of someone who is vindictive, depressed, hostile, or cold. Yet, if they happen to meet her, they search in vain for a living model of the portrait their patient has meticulously drawn. Instead of the vindictive, or depressed, or cold woman, they may find someone quite different. She may be thoughtful and reticent, but open and responsive rather than depressed. Or she may seem quietly joyous, deeply calm. Ruthellen Josselson writes about her habit of "grouchily" challenging therapists when they present a case in which a client is described as having an angry, controlling, narcissistic, envious, or emotionally neglectful mother. "You mean," she corrects, "the client experiences her mother as difficult."

It is those powerful experiences I describe. The way a son or daughter interacts with a mother, the way he or she perceives a mother, may be very different from another person's more objective account. Experiences are no less real or less compelling because they are subjective.

A fourth danger in exploring the subject of difficult mothers is that of appearing to add to the already endless list of instructions about how to be a good mother. Over the past hundred years, mothers have been bombarded with expert opinions on their parenting behavior. A book about difficult mothers risks appearing to offer further reminders to mothers of the harm they might do their child if they do not mother according to specific guidelines.

This book does not offer a list of what to do and what to avoid. Instead, it looks at two people in a powerful life-shaping relationship and describes the framework in which some people (about 20 percent of us) experience a mother as difficult. Their specific contexts and individual experiences are beyond the reach of broad generalizations. Some children have the genetic makeup of a hardy dandelion and are able to grow in rough conditions. Other children have the genetic makeup of an orchid, whose special sensitivities create special vulnerability. "Difficult mother" is not a simple definition. The term can be seen as shorthand for other terms I use, such as "difficult relationship" or "difficult relational environment." In that context I ask, "How does a mother's persistent criticism, resentment, neglect, rigidity, or volatility shape some children's minds and emotions?" I ask, "What are key differences between healthy conflicts and irritations, on the one hand, and, on the other, intractable patterns of conflict and tension that distort and constrain an entire relationship?" I describe how "key experiences" or events and words and actions come to build internal models for a son's or daughter's interpersonal world.

A discussion of difficult mothers is dangerous, too, because it may be misinterpreted as endorsing the myth that mothers are solely responsible for a child's well-being. Why, after all, am I focusing on mothers? Are not fathers equally responsible? Do not grandparents, siblings, friends, neighbors, teachers all have the potential to interact with and shape a child? My answer is, "Of course." Mothers are not the sole source of human understanding and support, but they play a major role, both in nature and in culture. While we develop through many experiences and many relationships, we tend to rely on and reflect on the satisfactions and frustrations of this primary relationship. Rarely do we cease to care about what our mother thinks of us and how she responds to us. However, because a father is often equally important, I sometimes use the term "parent" to suggest that the problems that people are somewhat more likely to experience with a mother may also apply to a difficult father.

For most parents and their children, the experience of belonging to one another has ups and downs, yet whatever the glitches, scuffles, and conflicts, the relationship is largely comforting and supportive. But what does it feel like to suffer more pain in a relationship than comfort and pleasure? What if a significant attachment is so confusing and disturbing that, in accepting it, we have to accept repeated criticism, derision, demands, intrusions, or anger? What if our daily words and acts are routinely distorted? What if we have to distrust ourselves or discount our own wishes or constantly police our thoughts and actions to secure a relationship that most people take for granted? It is in these circumstances that the term "difficult mother" must be understood.

The audience I have in mind consists of adults of all ages who are trying to make sense of their experiences. Some may puzzle over experiences in the distant past. Some may be grappling with continuing difficulties. Some readers will be parents who are trying to understand the bewildering distress of their own children. Some readers will be therapists and clinicians trying to improve the conceptual framework for troubled attachments. Some readers may be on the cusp of adulthood, seeking a vocabulary to shape their still-raw emotions. Many who search for understanding may function at a high level in many aspects of their lives, yet feel constrained and confused by the lingering effects of this difficult relationship. They may be silenced, too, in a culture that either idealizes or demonizes motherhood and leaves little room for the complex mix of feelings in which a kind of love is mixed with anger and outrage. One urge shared by the men and women who feel both wronged and confused is to articulate, understand, and manage the bewilderment and frustration of their paradoxical feelings.

IN CHAPTER ONE, "Difficult Mothers: Common Patterns," I introduce the emotional dilemma that sits at the heart of this difficult relationship. I then describe the broad categories into which difficult relationships fall. In Chapter Two, "The Science Behind a Mother's Power," I look at the latest research in developmental psychology and neuroscience that explains why a mother's role remains central in our emotional makeup. In the next five chapters, one by one, I describe different patterns of difficulty. Chapter Three, "The Angry Mother," looks at the impacts of a mother's emotional volatility and the consequences of dealing with her unpredictable, heated emotions. Chapter Four, "The Controlling Mother," looks at the impact of a mother's intrusiveness and inflexibility and common adaptations to these constraints. Chapter Five, "The Narcissistic Mother," describes the disturbing dilemma a child faces when he or she is required to shore up a mother's grandiose image. Chapter Six, "The Envious Mother," explores the dilemma a child faces when his or her successes seem to offend a mother. In Chapter Seven, "The Emotionally Unavailable Mother," I look at the tragic impact of a mother's emotional neglect, often caused by depression. These chapters end with suggestions for conducting your own "emotional audit." This audit provides practical tools for reviewing how a difficult relationship with a mother may continue to affect you. The audit includes exercises that should help identify both the defenses and the capabilities you might have developed to adapt to a difficult relationship. The audit then indicates strategies you might use for reshaping your responses and expectations.

In Chapter Eight, "Am I a Difficult Mother?" I highlight essential differences between normal tensions and disappointments within this primary relationship, on the one hand, and the cruel, confusing paradox of a difficult mother, on the other. In the final chapter, "Resilience," I show how the quality, coherence, and depth of understanding impact on the ability to manage and overcome the power of a difficult mother.

This book draws on a wide body of research—my own and that of others—including decades of observations of mothers and infants, clinical case histories, developmental theories, and new findings in the science of human attachment. I refer to my own research on young children's development, on mothers and teenagers, on early adulthood, and on midlife transitions. The case histories are based on interviews with men and women ranging in age from seventeen to sixty-seven. As interviewer, I explore the stories people tell of their experiences, how these are given meaning, and how meaning shapes their sense of self and their expectations of other people. I then conduct a thematic analysis of the transcripts and map out patterns within the different, unique experiences. Interpretation is developed further by reference to tried and tested theories of psychological development and of the lasting impacts of early attachment.

Over the past fifteen years I have conducted a series of interviews with 176 young people and adult men and women focusing on their experiences of being mothered. About 20 percent of the 176 women and men—35 total, 19 women and 16 men—gave accounts that clearly depict a difficult relational environment generated and maintained by a mother's behavior. The participants came from a range of races and ethnic groups and from two countries, the United States and the United Kingdom. Because I do not make generalizations about groups of people, I do not normally specify the race or ethnicity of the participants. I do, however, note the ages of the people speaking, since views of a mother and her impact on our lives tend to change as we ourselves change.

It is not known to what extent these findings represent the general population. Nor is there a statistical assessment of the probabilities of either damage or resilience from the distinctive experience of a difficult mother. The aim of this qualitative research is not to count up the number of people who have difficult mothers but to understand those who do and to identify common patterns that can help them and others make sense of their experiences.

This approach rests on my belief that a person is someone who lives and develops in relatedness to others. Early experiences of being tended, attached, and *seen*, in a very broad sense, by our earliest caregiver—who is usually a mother—help construct our sense of self and our capacity to reflect on our emotions and to understand others' responses to us. When we experience prolonged difficulty in making ourselves known and feeling the warmth of another person's understanding, we try to gain what comfort we can by reshaping ourselves and denying our needs. In order to manage this difficult dilemma, we have to understand and reformulate its terms. My readers will judge whether this book presents a helpful working model.

DIFFICULT MOTHERS

Chapter One

DIFFICULT MOTHERS: COMMON PATTERNS

"Who has a difficult mother?"

I POSE THIS question to a group of teenage girls. They exchange looks and laughter, then raise their hands high, as each competes with the others to claim the *most* difficult mother. Some of the thirteen- and fourteen-year-old girls bounce in their seats, eager to speak out about their frustration. Clara complains that her mother "treats me like a little girl—still." Gina's words cut across those of her friend: "I feel smothered by my mom. She wants to wrap me up and keep me safe." A third girl, Amanda, says, "My mom doesn't have a clue who I am."

The sixteen-year-olds are more cautious. They look around to see who might share their irritation. "I won't be able to have any fun and just do what I want until she dies," exclaims Magda. An older girl, Lia, age eighteen and on the cusp of adulthood, is more resigned. "Whatever," she shrugs. "I'm leaving home soon." And seventeen-year-old Sarah tops them all: "I need an exit strategy to keep sane."

In another room, at another time, I pose this question to a group of fifteen grown women—the mothers of the teenage girls. They, too, catch one another's eyes and nod knowingly. They acknowledge a common burden: the mix of irritation and amusement, the residue of past arguments, the unease of remaining dependence. Suddenly one woman gasps and exclaims, "I hope I don't turn out to be just like her." Uneasy laughter spreads like a wave across the room. "I hope my children don't feel about me the way I felt about my mother," we hear, and the laughter ceases. There are sighs, murmurs, followed by a cold pause in which they consider this possibility.

On a different occasion, I address a group of twenty men. There is no sudden surge of group feeling, only uneasy expectation. The room rings with silence. Some look down and avoid others' gaze. Some shift position in their seats. Others stiffen. A few cross their arms against their chest and look coolly ahead. Some shake their heads, but a few nod thoughtfully, and one braces against the back of his chair as he speaks. "Yes. I have a difficult mother. Very difficult." The others in the group then turn to him and acknowledge his confession. Some shrug; some nod.

In each of the different settings, one person's story sparks another's. Some recall snatches of memory, peripheral, newly discovered. Some are fixed vignettes, frequently visited in private thoughts, probed like a tongue searching out a sore tooth. The different narratives dovetail. Some describe dramas of neglect, some of criticism and punishment. Some complaints merge with amusing anecdotes about embarrassment or disappointment that follow normal ups and downs of a close relationship, while others reveal a persistent, demanding emotional environment that marks a child and shapes an adult who has a difficult mother.

Different Difficulties

Many people utter casual complaints about a mother. Teenage girls bond over conversations about an "impossible mother." They mark out new distance from their families. They are independent people with their own perspective, their own norms. They are eager to deny their dependence and to imagine fresh parent-free identities. Among women, too, a distinctive tone sounds when they talk about their mothers; they expect that others will understand the tension and the affection, the pull of duty and the grind of irritation. For teenage boys, who rarely talk about their mothers, the word "mother" carries an embarrassing emotional heft. They try to marginalize her importance and mock her tenderness.

Complaining about mothers is a common social activity. Sometimes we complain because we are uneasy with the power she has over us. Sometimes high expectations lead us to make impossible demands of her, and disappointment is inevitable. Our need for a mother's attention and appreciation and understanding is great; we tend to be critical of responses that are not precisely what we hope for, and we complain when she does not fully meet our needs.

The intimate history of our love and dependence makes it unlikely that we objectively weigh a mother's qualities. Because her words and actions have such a powerful effect, we often cannot distinguish in the heat of the moment between a specific act that has hurt us and a pattern of behavior that has defeated us. Common shortcomings—perhaps her repeated reminders for you to "be careful," or her compulsive checking-up questions about your health and happiness, or her mismatched clothes that you feel reflect badly on you, or her gushing smile that makes you feel like a kid when you want to feel like a grown-up—are embarrassing. Perhaps she thinks you need her to look after you, when you see yourself as independent. Perhaps in her presence an earlier, more dependent self is reawakened and you come to doubt your own maturity.

A mother's concern may be more irritating than comforting. When you are ill, her anxiety can make you feel worse. She reminds you of every precaution you should take and asks what seem to you like a hundred questions to get an update on your condition. When you have a setback, such as losing a job, her concern may aggravate your own anxiety. Her sympathy sends the message that you might not be able to deal with this disappointment, when you want to believe that you can. Her persistent questions ("How are you feeling?" and "Any news?")—whether these are about your health and happiness, your love life, your career, or your creature comforts—focus on susceptibilities you'd rather ignore. Her attempts to reassure or compliment you may annoy you beyond measure. Maternal affection and interest catapult you back to the child who requires her support and sympathy, whom you believe you've left behind. Ordinary mothers are sometimes "difficult" in this loose sense because they call up contextual memories that frustrate us with our own feelings of dependence and dissatisfaction. So when we complain about a mother's imperfections, it is important to remember that we rather than she may be at fault.

The important concept of a "good-enough" mother registers

the simple fact that a mother does not have to be perfect, does not have to produce the right response to every claim or need of her child. A good-enough mother is a mother with whom a son or daughter finds more comfort than pain, more resonance than dissonance. A good-enough mother has an ordinary person's foibles and fallibility but nonetheless introduces her child to the multiple transactions that constitute love between two imperfect people, each of whose engagement with the other coexists with their own thoughts, needs, desires, and distractions. A good-enough mother may have habits that are more often annoying than endearing. She may slip into infuriatingly outdated assumptions about her child's interests and abilities; but she is good-enough because the relationship she offers has room for understanding, imagination, growth, and pleasure.

Snapshots of Difficult Mothers

So what is a difficult mother?

The best definition of a difficult mother is someone who presents her child with the dilemma: "Either develop complex and constricting coping mechanisms to maintain a relationship with me on my own terms, or suffer ridicule, disapproval, or rejection."

In the following snapshots of mothers and children, we can begin to mark out the differences between a mother who generally offers warmth and comfort, and a mother who imposes terms of engagement that prohibit us from enjoying love and simultaneously attending to our own needs.

SNAPSHOT ONE: BEWARE OF MY ANGER.

Seth, age twenty-four, is on constant alert for signs of anger:

I can't mark out what sets it off. Not even after all these years of trying to think it through. There's neither rhyme nor reason, as far as I can see. The best I can do is see it coming, a couple of minutes before, maybe even before she feels it. Her neck starts to thicken, and her arms sort of pull in tight against her ribs, and when you see the color deepening in her chest and spreading upward, you know you have to brace yourself. I guess we all have a temper, but Mother's is awesome to behold. If you don't somehow duck it, you can end up with a black eye. But it's not only the worry about getting out without a smack. It's also just—being on the receiving end of this, and what it does to you, what it says about who you are.

SNAPSHOT TWO: YOU'RE BAD IF YOU DON'T PLEASE ME.

Kenny, age thirty-two, describes a key experience with his mother:

When things are going well, she has a sweetness that's like a song. Everything smooth and easy. She's generous and ready to please you. She's full of praise for you. But say no to her just once, no matter how small you try to make that "no," and the world turns. She glares. She won't talk, unless it's an eruption of complaints and accusations and here and there a threat. Like, the other day she said, "There's that nasty streak in you, I was hoping it maybe was gone, and there it is. Nasty to the core." I love her to bits and hope one day I'll get the hang of just when it's okay to speak my mind and when I just have to cut everything else from my mind and do what Mom asks. I'm hoping to get that gist, but I'm not there yet. So it's lookout time, even when she's running on sweet. You gotta be careful, otherwise you're in the place with all the walls closing in on you.

SNAPSHOT THREE: MY NEEDS COME FIRST.

Jenna, age fourteen, focuses on her mother's needs:

I have to watch out for her. It makes me, you know, less selfish, more mature, than my friends. They're thinking, "What do I want to do? I'm gonna do that. How do I get around my mom to do that?" But for me, it's more like, "Can this fit in around what I have to do for her?" She's a real good mom, and very loving, but she can only take so much. I'm so happy when she's okay. I'm good at seeing what she needs and sorting things so she doesn't get overwhelmed. As long as I keep on my toes, she can be happy for long stretches.

SNAPSHOT FOUR: YOUR HAPPINESS HURTS ME.

Rachel, age twenty-seven, is discouraged by her mother's responses to the good things in her life. She describes "the gloom that descends over [my mother] when I'm obviously happy." She notes

the hardness of her mouth and manner that sets in when I tell her something good about my day. Even getting into college and getting a part scholarship—she starts chewing her lips and ruminating on disasters, when I thought I was bringing her something like a present that would warm and cheer her. It drains the pleasure from everything, and I wonder why I ever bother.

SNAPSHOT FIVE: FAILURE TO SEE.

Sonia holds her seven-month-old son on her lap, with baby Kieran's head facing away, his eyes roaming the empty distance. When Kieran wriggles to a different position, Sonia holds him down and pins the baby's arms to his lap. Then she begins to raise and lower the baby's arms, once, twice, three times, giving them the appearance of a doll's limited range of movement. She puts Kieran in his cot, on his back. The baby's eyes fix on Sonia's face, and his hands reach up. Sonia hands the baby a rattle. When Kieran drops it, starts to fuss, and twists his head toward his mother, Sonia sighs, puts a pacifier in the baby's mouth, and turns her head, gazing at the opposite wall.

These five snapshots show very different images of a difficult mother, but each depicts a paradox confronting a son or daughter who must comply with tough terms as he or she seeks closeness, comfort, and understanding.

The Difficult Dilemma

All parents have ups and downs. All parents have bad days. A few bouts of anger, a smattering of unreasonable demands, occasional neediness, a careless or vicious word, do not make a difficult mother. In a significant psychological sense, a difficult mother is a great deal more than a mother who is sometimes difficult. Though difficult mothers come in many different guises, there is an underlying pattern. A difficult mother is one who presents her child with the dilemma: "Either develop complex and constricting coping mechanisms to maintain a relationship with me, at great cost to your own outlook, imagination, and values, or suffer ridicule, disapproval, or rejection."

A child cannot easily escape this dilemma. A child does not have the option to say, "I don't care whether you think I'm bad" or "I don't care whether you notice me" or "I don't care whether you are angry or disapproving." A child is terrified at the prospect of being abandoned. The primitive panic at abandonment lasts long after the physical helplessness of the infant ends. Even as adults, we are rarely willing to renounce a mother's love even when it brings pain, frustration, and disappointment.

Children work hard to acquire special strategies to manage the emotional environment they inhabit. The strategies required with a difficult mother are very different from the interpersonal skills most children develop in their families as they exchange affection and anger, play and compete, test and negotiate their place within the family. The particular strategies a difficult mother imposes on a child are ruled by fear, anxiety, and confusion. While most children learn rules of behavior through a fairly broad spectrum of praise and admonishment and forgiveness, those with difficult mothers walk a tightrope in dreadful anticipation of the cost of any slipup. They inhabit a high-risk world that requires anxious vigilance of the mother's responses. This is her legacy, and it often shapes her child's sense of self and relationships with others, long after the "child" has left home.

The Raw Experience

Over a century ago, Leo Tolstoy wrote the opening sentence of his novel *Anna Karenina*, which marks a crucial difference in the emotional atmosphere of different families: "Happy families are all alike; every unhappy family is unhappy in its own way." We grasp immediately the difference between human interactions that flow smoothly, with grace, joy, and humor, and human interactions that stick, stop, and start up again in bizarre ways. In a so-called happy family, conversation makes sense and moves forward; smiles, laughter, looks of sympathy or sorrow, exclamations of surprise or dismay are exchanged. Inevitably, there are hesitations, misunderstandings, disagreements, and confusions. Arguments erupt in every family, but in most cases the disturbance is transient. Views are aired with passion, perspectives are reconsidered, hurt feelings are soothed, and comfortable interactions are soon restored.

When the conversation breaks apart, when one person's voice is picked up and picked over in ways that confuse and enrage, when expressions of tenderness or calls for sympathy are ignored or ridiculed, when you keep an anxious lookout for eruptions of anger or intrusive, implacable commands, when what you offer as an explanation or a gesture of connection is used as a weapon against you— then you have entered the distinctive territory of the unhappy family. Instead of clearing the air, arguments release new conflicts that hang there, heavy and ominous. You can see things going awry, though it is difficult to identify precisely what is wrong. Interactions have familiar patterns but make no sense. When you seek clarification, you meet with confusion. When you try to soothe someone, you trigger another outburst. You try to explain and defend yourself, but your efforts are flung back at you, distorted and mixed with new accusations. These incoherent and uncomfortable exchanges are instantly recognizable as the dynamics of an unhappy family. In this respect, Tolstoy's saying could be transposed, as it was by Nabokov, for all unhappy families are pretty much alike.

Descriptions of the dilemma posed by a difficult mother have a chilling familiarity. Whether a son or daughter is aged six years or sixty years, they talk about a relational environment in which the parent's needs take priority and a child's will is harnessed to a parent's. The difficult mother is likely to use a son's or daughter's continuing need for her care, love, approval, and interest to control or manipulate a child, and to use a child's attempts to reshape the relationship as weapons against him or her.

Once the dilemma becomes embedded in your relationship, a single word or gesture can bring it to the fore. You then switch into a new gear, a special gear your gut knows well. You are primed to defend yourself and to placate her, or to withdraw, by either running from the room or emptying your mind. Her anger or demands or disapproval require your full attention. Whatever your plans, whatever your mood, whatever your private preoccupations may have been a few moments before, they have to be recalibrated. If your mother is not appeased, if her dictates are not followed, if her needs are not met, you face the darkness of abandonment, the terror of attack. You may feel "invaded" by her voice, stifled by her demands, confused by a barrage of "reasoning" that lacks coherence but insists on being heard. Though your goals narrow to emotional survival of the present crisis, you feel outrage and anger and a heated wish to change this system of interaction so that you can be heard, so that your views can be expressed and your feelings acknowledged.

But you swallow that wish and hold it firmly in your silent core. By this time, you probably know what the outcome of any attempt at negotiation is likely to be. It is your mother, not you, who dictates how things should be interpreted. When you express your views, you stoke the flames of discord. If your perspective is incompatible with her perspective, then yours should be blown away like dust. If you try to maintain your own perspective, you will meet with derision or ridicule. Your attempts to defend and justify yourself, your pleas for understanding, your craving for independence, are all targets for attack. They stimulate a frisson of rage or despair, and accumulate as evidence that you are completely wrong and she is completely right. The system of communication closes down. Whatever she delivers, you deserve. Whatever she demands is justified.

How different this is from the positive, mutual relationship that most mother/child pairs enjoy! Each checks in with the other, updates information, and explores the other's inner world. Normally, this intimate relationship is both active and flexible. Learning about being with other people involves awareness that you have an impact on their responses and that you can shape their view of you. This dynamic is an important part of what makes a relationship real and also a part of how we develop our sense of self. Another's responses give us information about who we are, but we also give them information, which they re-present to us, showing that they "get" us. But in a difficult relational environment, we monitor another person not because we are likely to be rewarded but because we are on guard. "Am I in trouble with this person?" and "Have I done something to ruin this relationship?" and "Is she going to hurt me?"

Sometimes you may forget her consummate skills in enforcing this dilemma. Perhaps she seems to be relenting: her anger has cooled; she seems more flexible, willing to enjoy your success and acknowledge your views. So you approach her with hope and joy in your heart; maybe this time you'll find the right way to elicit a positive response. When you fail, when she ignores you or condemns you, you conclude that you have no power to shape this relationship. Her skewed responses, her lack of focus, her inability to pick up your emotional cues are bewildering and frustrating. During the first-stage response you lose faith in your own perspective. You lose faith in your ability to communicate what you feel. You give up on making yourself known, seen, understood altogether. You forgo recognition of your needs. Trapped within the difficult dilemma, you may cease to be mindful of your own thoughts and feelings.

In the second stage, you cling to patterns of interaction that on some occasions in the past have generated some reward and less punishment. If she is responsive only when you are quiet, or only when you are dependent, or only when you are failing, or only when you are succeeding, you will develop these roles and these qualities only. You remain on constant alert for signs that the dilemma is springing back to the foreground.

Finally, you set aside the hope of bringing your own voice into the relationship. You concentrate on meeting the terms of the dilemma. You may adapt by placating a parent's anger, or mastering your fear of her anger by shutting down all feeling in yourself. You may become primed for quick compliance with every demand, or you may appear compliant while secretly plotting escape and revenge. You may put on a show of competence to meet your mother's needs, but suffer a sense of helplessness. You may eschew success because you have learned that this threatens your mother, or you may become a defiantly high-achiever. You manage day-to-day life with a difficult mother, yet take great care to select what you reveal about yourself.

Five Common Patterns of Difficulty

This quandary will be instantly recognizable by anyone who grew up in a difficult relational environment. Though the specific context is unique for each person, confusion, coercion, and a sense of chaos are its common features. While we may not ever be able to obliterate the past from our present life, seeing broad patterns in difficult interpersonal dynamics offers insight, and insight is key to overcoming their negative power. There are five categories of "difficult mother" or difficult relational environments generated by our experience of a central dilemma. Each category has distinctive styles of control, distinctive justifications, distinctive demands, and distinctive threats.

Anger

The most common and most direct means of enforcing a difficult relational dilemma is through anger. A parent uses anger to control, threaten, and define a child.

All parents get angry sometimes, and nearly all children are distressed by a parent's anger, whether it is occasional and transient or frequent and persistent. Parents get angry when they are tired, under stress, or at their wits' end as to how to deal with a child. They may use the semblance of anger to get a quick response when a child puts himself in danger. "Don't touch that!" a parent shouts as a child reaches toward a boiling kettle, and the child cries in terror at the tone of the parent's voice, indifferent to the burn he has narrowly escaped. Anger also signals disapproval and is a primitive form of moral teaching. The sharp dark tone of an angry voice signals, "This is wrong" and "I disapprove of that."

Anger is part of normal family life. Because children find a parent's anger so uncomfortable, they work hard to learn what triggers it. This is one way they learn about the many facets of acceptable behavior. They practice managing a parent's anger by showing that they are sad or contrite, or by dissipating it with charm. Anger becomes part of their play routine, as one doll or action figure shouts, scolds, and threatens before either beating up or making up. Children talk to themselves about who is "mad" or "cross" and who is "being bad." Anger—their own and their parents'—is something to notice, consider, and manage.

However, when a parent's anger is violent and unpredictable, a child cannot learn rules for avoiding it. In some relational environments, anger dominates parent/child interactions. Then, whether dormant or active, anger shadows everything. Children in this environment are always on the alert for emotional explosions. They can make no sense of the connection between their behavior and a parent's anger—and often there is none, for in the guise of reasonable punishment or discipline, a parent may use a child as a means to discharge her own pent-up rage that may actually have more to do with her life situation than with anything her child has done. The child may be told, "I am angry because you've done something wrong," but in truth the child is simply a target for a parent's frustration and discontent.

Prolonged stress generated by a parent's unpredictable anger has a physiological impact on a child that then lowers his or her tolerance for stress. When a child is flooded with unremitting anxiety, the young brain forms fewer of the mental circuits needed to regulate emotional states. The awful irony is that children who most need to acquire the skill to soothe themselves and control their responses may be the least well equipped to do so. Long-term stress is toxic to the young brain and impairs its key task: learning how to integrate and regulate thoughts and emotions.

Sometimes a child defends himself by dissociation. The thought "Mommy's angry" is disconnected from all feeling. The pain inflicted by a parent's anger—with its associations of disapproval, the implicit threat of abandonment, and the signal of danger—is managed by constructing a "stone wall" defense: turn yourself into a stone wall and you won't feel anything. But as a stone wall, you also do not understand or even acknowledge your own feelings.

Another child may remain constantly alert to her mother's anger. Danger is ever-present. Even in the apparent security of her home, she feels helpless in the face of unpredictable attacks. An overwhelming sense of shame may result, stemming from the belief that this suffering is deserved. Some children, witnessing a mother's being overwhelmed by anger, are then unable to regulate their own emotions. A "prolonged state of high arousal"—or sense of danger—impairs a child's ability to learn about herself and others.

Control

A second category of a difficult mother is the controlling mother. All parents have to manage a child, teach a child, and influence a child's behavior. A child needs parents to articulate right from wrong, to identify what is acceptable and what is objectionable. A child needs parents to stand by as he or she learns how to tolerate frustration and disappointment. Raising a child involves a great deal of control and persuasion and example-setting, but there is a difference between control in the form of necessary discipline and socialization, and control that eats away at a child's individuality.

A controlling mother imposes highly specific expectations about who a child should be and what he should (or should not) achieve, think, and feel. Often a controlling mother defends her inflexibility as a sign of certainty and guidance. But inflexibility is destructive when incorporated into the structure of mother/

child interaction, wherein a mother is the sole authority on the legitimacy of a child's own experiences. An inflexible mother may appeal to high principles as she refuses to listen or learn from her child, but what she in fact does is discount her child's experience and knowledge.

To accommodate a mother's control, a son or daughter may suppress their real thoughts, feelings, and even their own sense of being someone with independent desires and needs. Choices become irrelevant because acting according to the child's preferences threatens the relationship with her mother. The child sees little point even in identifying her own desires, because "This is what I want" has no meaning to the person who matters most.

A mother's inflexibility makes genuine communication impossible or irrelevant. Some people find other listeners and develop self-reflection and self-expression through close connections with others, such as a father, sibling, friend, teacher, or lover. But there remains a sense of profound betrayal: "Why does my mother, whose responses mean so much, refuse to listen to me?" and "Why does my mother, who claims to love me, try to shape me into something I'm not?"

Narcissism and Envy

The third and fourth categories of a difficult mother are set within two related mind-sets: narcissism and envy. In a narcissistic environment, a mother imposes on her child the task of becoming a mirror that flatters and glorifies her. The child is valued insofar as he or she supports the mother's shaky self-esteem. The dilemma is: "Either admire me, and confirm my grandiose fantasies, or I'll see you as an inferior person who is of little use to me." A child forgoes his own needs and becomes a footstool to his mother. Or a child is given the mission of satisfying his mother's narcissistic needs by proxy; but because these needs are unrealistic and unstable, no success will satisfy her. In this role, the child is likely to feel forever a failure.

Envy is one of the most confusing and disturbing maternal responses a child can experience. In this dilemma, success poses a danger to the relationship. Envy is a strange, often unacknowledged response that arises from resentment at another's happiness or achievement. Sometimes a child's joy or imagination can spark a mother's envy as easily as success can. A mother's unspoken thoughts are, "Why should she experience joy when I do not?" and "Why should she exercise imagination and curiosity when my vision is so limited?" and "Why should she enjoy optimism when I feel so frustrated?" Since envy is usually directed toward someone with whom we compare ourselves, a daughter is more likely to be the object of a mother's envy than is a son. "She has no right to delight in who she is when I take no pleasure in myself," is the attitude that underlies envy. As a child comes to realize that a parent cannot take delight in what delights the child, a pall is cast over all pleasure.

Neglect

A fifth category of a difficult mother involves various forms of neglect. "Neglect" covers a wide range of behavior. There is neglect by omission, in which a parent lacks interest in a child. There are extreme cases of neglect to care for a child that involve systematic cruelty, as when a child is denied food and freedom of movement and education and medical care. Sometime neglect arises from a mother's addiction or substance abuse. The child then lives in chaos as a mother's cravings dominate their daily lives. Here the dilemma is: "Either take care of me and see to your own needs, or we will all be destroyed by my inability to function." Children who become the caregiver may appear mature and controlled, but they often feel helpless and frightened. Their competence is achieved at the cost of youthful curiosity and exploration.

Another cause of neglect is depression. A depressed mother is a difficult mother because she is disengaged and nonresponsive. Here the dilemma may be shaped by a child's fantasy that there is something he or she might do to lift a mother's spirits. However unintentionally, a mother's unhappiness or incapacity poses the following dilemma: "Either develop strategies to heal me, or I'll disappear." A mother's depression may feel to a child like emotional death.

Contexts and Conditions

When a relationship goes wrong, the difficulty is unlikely to be caused by one person alone. A difficult relationship emerges as two or more people come together and interact and find mutual resonance or dissonance. A mother becomes "difficult," just as a child becomes "difficult," within a dynamic context in which two people are passionately connected, influence each other's responses, and interpret each other's responses in different ways. Some mothers have personalities and habits that increase their probability of having a difficult relationship with any child, but often two children with the same mother have very different experiences of her. One sibling remains calm in the face of a mother's outbursts whereas another cowers in terror. One child triggers a mother's anger or dependence while another evokes empathy and patience. A mother may demand subservience from a daughter but not from a son; she may pressure one child to conform rigidly to her ambitious expectations but allow another to go her own way. A mother may expect one child to be her caregiver while she offers support to another. The same mother may be difficult or good-enough for her different children.

Gender, personality, birth order all moderate this complex, interactive bond. Genes, too, moderate the emotional environment. A child who carries the "hardy dandelion" gene may be resilient to the moods, volatility, and disapproval of a parent, while a sibling who carries the "orchid" gene will be more vulnerable to difficult circumstances. This child may be highly reactive to fear, so that even small and fleeting signs of anger promote intense anxiety. The emotional environment is very different for different children with the same mother.

Mothers themselves undergo change and growth. One mother may foster a comfortable emotional environment for a four-year-old child who remains compliant and eager to please, but be a difficult mother to a fourteen-year-old who criticizes and opposes her. One mother may show appreciation and trust and support to a thirty-year-old daughter, but when that same daughter was fifteen years old, the mother's own self-doubts triggered anger and control. However, some relationships remain difficult throughout a person's life. Some relationships that were difficult only in one phase of a child's life may have a continuing impact. Even a mother's death may not release her child from the constraints and pain of the dilemma she imposed.

THE QUALITY OF our relationship with our mother impacts our well-being long after we have left the family home, long after we have become independent. Though difficult childhood experiences stay with us, they do not fix forever our emotions, our thought patterns, or our mental life. Many people who have had very difficult relationships with their mother are high-functioning people. Many achieve confidence and competence in varied walks of life. Many people have developed competence *because* of a difficult relationship with a mother. At the same time, they are likely to grapple with powerful feelings of anger and protest that instinctively they know are legitimate but that intellectually they may be reluctant to explore and accept. The struggle to make sense of and articulate these experiences often founders on the *incoherence* that so frequently accompanies difficult relationships. It is sometimes preferable for a person to ignore a problem than to struggle with the confusion of addressing it. The aim of this book is to make understanding possible, to present new ways of reflecting on old wounds, and to show that at any age new strategies for managing this difficult dilemma can be achieved.

Chapter Two

THE SCIENCE BEHIND A MOTHER'S POWER

The Young Brain

W HEN WE experience a mother as difficult, we do so in the context of her importance to us. The way we see and value ourselves is influenced by her view of us. How we expect others to behave toward us is in part a function of early interactions with our closest family members. Recent findings in brain science have deepened our understanding of a mother's pervasive influence. Our relationship with her becomes a model for all intimate relationships. It shapes the circuits of our infant brain—circuits that are used to understand and manage our own emotions and to "read" other people's thoughts and feelings. When we see how our sense of self is developed in relationship to her, we can also see why, when she is difficult, we may feel that we are losing our mind.

In all observed cultures, in all recorded times, human infants engage intimately with the person who cares for them; and in all recorded times, in all observed cultures, the parent whose introduces an infant to the interpersonal world of love and dependence is a mother. A mother and baby lock together in a mutual gaze, each looking back to the other. This early, prolonged eye contact is so important to the growing human brain that evolution has left nothing to chance. A brain-stem reflex ensures that the baby turns to look at the mother's face.

Until recently, so-called experts on babies advised parents that babies could not really see a mother and that babies had no concept of what a person was for many months or even years after their first all-absorbing introduction to their mother; but new findings show something very different. The areas of the brain that adults use to recognize and respond to faces are active from birth. From the moment a baby looks into his mother's face, he sees a person. He sees someone who expresses feelings and whose expressions show responses to him. This interaction triggers high levels of hormones that flood the infant with pleasure. These "endogenous opiates"—naturally occurring chemicals that block pain and produce pleasure—are a healthy version of external opiates such as heroin. They reward the infant as he engages in the primary lessons of vital interpersonal relationships.

Sight is only one trigger for these pleasure-inducing chemicals. Newborns orient their heads to the sound of their mother's voice, and they rapidly learn to recognize and follow its tone and rhythm. They stare longer at an image if it smells like their mother. The instinct a mother has to hold her baby on her left side (which is wired to the right side of the brain) facilitates right-hemisphere to right-hemisphere communication, the part of the brain that specializes in the emotional self. As she cradles the baby on her left side, she communicates with the infant's right brain and the infant's behavior stimulates the mother's right brain. Even negative experiences of fear can positively stimulate a baby's emotional growth; when the "fight-or-flight" system is activated, the rate of breathing increases, along with the heart rate and blood pressure; but as a mother soothes a troubled infant, he feels the ebb of negative emotions and has his first lessons in the crucial task of regulating his own emotions.

Learning and Loving

We begin living in a relationship with our mother at birth, as we experience with life-sustaining vividness what it is like to be held, fed, soothed, and warmed. But our experiences go far beyond these practical details because infants also experience a mother's responses to their inner states. This is the beginning of our understanding of the mind—both our own and others'.

One of our most basic needs is making sense of other people's responses to us. Before babies can walk or talk or even crawl, they can tell the difference between expressions of happiness and sadness and anger. For example, they can recognize that a happy-looking face with a smile and crinkly eyes goes with the chirp of a happy tone of voice. The newborn's brain, primed to attend, absorb, and learn from human contact, undergoes a growth spurt during the first eighteen months of life by which time the right hemisphere of the brain shapes the pathways for social and emotional learning.

It isn't only the infant's brain that changes. As she engages with her infant, a mother's brain, too, is stimulated to new growth and learning. Mothers of newborns are often said to be simply obsessed by their baby. Once their intense focus was put down to pregnancy-related hormones, but new brain-imaging techniques show actual brain changes brought on by interaction with infants. In response to an infant's cries and laughter, for example, the parent's brain activity reveals a special pattern. In addition, the complex brain structures that control our emotions—the limbic system—undergo structural changes as we engage in parenting behavior. These changes increase a mother's ability to pick up cues from her infant.

As mother and baby interact, each gets smarter. In healthy situations, each is engrossed by the sights, sounds, and movements of the other; each is hungry to learn the other's language. Their mutual focus is so intricately coordinated that it has been described as an elaborate flowing dance wherein the participating partners get to know each other and get to know themselves through each other. Human psychology as we know it begins in this primary relationship. A passionate and absorbing bond with his or her primary caregiver, who is almost always the mother, is the infant's first experience of loving and of being one person in a loving pair.

A Mother's Focus and Flirtation

An intriguing picture of the long, complex, and flexible series of interactions, contact, stimulation, and delight that form early interpersonal "conversations" is revealed in films of mothers and their babies. They gaze at each other like romantic lovers in an activity called "eye love" because of the mutual watching and the quick rush of reward each has in seeing the face of the other. The nonsense babbling that mothers speak to a baby is actually a profound conversation. The baby responds with coos to a mother's coos. The baby gestures in rhythm with the mother's voice. Alison Gopnik describes this coordinated mutual excitement as "flirting": "When you talk, the baby is still; when you pause, the baby takes her turn and there's a burst of waving fists and kicking legs. . . . Like grown-up flirtation, baby flirtation bypasses language and establishes a more direct link between people."

Periods of exquisite responsiveness to each gesture and sound are interspersed with intervals, sometimes only a few seconds long, of solitude, and the baby's face turns away and the hectic responsiveness subsides. Such stimulation eventually is exhausting, and the baby needs "time out" to rest and absorb these rapid-fire exchanges. The baby's limb movements speed up but lose expressiveness. The rhythm of the baby's breathing changes. There are hectic efforts to suck a hand, and a jerking motion as the head wrests itself away from the mother's face. Sometimes the baby's back arches in an effort to move away. These cues—that the baby is overloaded or tired—are usually picked up by a mother. Normally, she sits back, eases her engagement, and watches her baby quietly until the baby indicates by some look or sound or gesture that he wants to reengage.

What happens if a mother does not respond? When that normal face-to-face interaction between mother and baby is interrupted—when the mother's face becomes frozen, still, or unresponsive—within minutes the baby becomes distressed. Even at the age of two months a baby will protest by wriggling, fretting, and bellowing if his mother's face is cold and unresponsive. The baby seems outraged that his signals are ignored. It is not easy to soothe a baby who has experienced this interruption in the relational conversation.

The Reference Point of Love

These early interactions form a reference point for what each of us seeks in people we love: to be seen and understood. Children form many relationships with other relatives and with friends that impact on their lives, but the emotional signaling between infant and mother forms the core sense of being a person with feelings who can communicate feelings to others. A key experience of having a difficult mother, whether we are three months old or thirty years old, is of the negative of that positive eye-to-eye engagement. With a difficult mother, our efforts to shape our mother's view are constantly frustrated. We feel ignored, erased, annihilated. We doubt who we are and what we feel. Perhaps our signals are interpreted as "bad" or "mean" or "selfish." We then inhabit a world of shame in which being known entails criticism and derision.

Children work hard to make sense of their interpersonal experiences. "Who is reliable?" and "Who offers me warmth and comfort and feeding?" and "Whose touch and smell and voice are associated with these?" are questions intricately linked to their survival. As the rudimentary sense of "self" and "other person" becomes more sophisticated, so do questions about their meanings: "What does that behavior indicate about me?" and "Does the person I'm trying to communicate with understand me?" and "Do my feelings resonate with others?" and "Am I really communicating?"

We continue to be particularly vulnerable to a mother's responses, even as we develop very different bonds with other people who see and discover us in different ways. For most parents and their children, the experience of belonging to each other has ups and downs, but whatever the trip-ups and scrapes along the way, the relationship is largely comforting, supportive, and expansive.

But what does it feel like to suffer more pain in a relationship than comfort and pleasure? What if those profound experiences of connection and embeddedness are so uncomfortable that, in reaching out for comfort and security, we are restricted and punished? What if we have to distrust ourselves or discount our own wishes or constantly police our thoughts and actions to gain comfort from the person we depend on? When this dilemma shapes a son's or daughter's experience of a mother, I use the shorthand of "difficult mother" to refer to a relationship that has many parts and many contexts and perspectives.

A Closer Look at Snapshots of Difficult Mothers

We can now look again at the snapshots of difficult mothers shown in Chapter One. At first glance they were intuitively recognizable as snapshots of a difficult mother, but the explanations here of how early relational experiences shape the emotional centers of our brain deepen understanding as to where difficulties lie.

SNAPSHOT ONE: BEWARE OF MY ANGER.

In this snapshot we saw Seth, age twenty-four, unable to find any "rhyme or reason" to his mother's temper, which "is awesome to behold." He wonders "what it says about who you are."

Unable to anticipate or understand his mother's anger, Seth is

always alert. His sense of danger is embedded in his past childhood dependence on his mother. To manage this stressful environment, he observes her closely. A small change in the color of
her skin or tension in her muscles or constriction in the pupils of
her eyes alerts him to potential danger. Sometimes people who
fear a parent become skilled in reading the internal states of others. This skill is useful in some contexts, but Seth's hypersensitivity to his mother's anger severely limits their relationship.

SNAPSHOT TWO: YOU'RE BAD IF YOU DON'T PLEASE ME.

Kenny, age thirty-two, describes a key experience with his
mother as turning on a dime: One minute she is full of praise,
"but say 'no' to her just once, and the world turns." Complaints
and accusations erupt, and he is told he is "nasty to the core."

Kenny is an independent adult, but his mother's disapproval
can put him in "the place with all the walls closing in on you."
He cannot bring any thoughts or desires that are different from
his mother's into the conversation (in the broadest sense) without being excoriated.

As a child he looked to his mother to "mirror" him. Did her
face harden with disapproval when he roughhoused with a friend?
Was it pinched with anxiety when he ran to meet the bus? Could
he speak his mind and see that she wanted to understand him?
What was her response to his growth and change? These past
responses are contained in his present vulnerability. Her disapproval shifts his entire sense of self from "good" to "bad." As a
result, he tries to avoid ever saying no to her.

Kenny confronts a paradox: the person he loves withdraws
warmth and approval if he does not toe the line she draws. He
hopes that "one day I'll get the hang of just when it's okay to
speak my mind and when I just have to cut everything else from

my mind and do what Mom asks." This type of paradox has been described by the psychologist Carol Gilligan as giving up on a relationship in order to preserve the relationship. You give up genuine communication for a feeling of comfort, but then you lose the comfort of real communication. Kenny gives up on forging a relationship in which he is seen and understood in order to avoid abuse.

SNAPSHOT THREE: MY NEEDS COME FIRST.

Jenna, age fourteen, who focuses on her mother's needs, has a harmonious relationship with her mother, but it is "difficult" because Jenna believes that to maintain such harmony she has to deny her own needs and impulses. She limits what she reveals of her own feelings for her mother's sake. Jenna's capacity to control her emotions and to empathize with others suggests that, as a baby, when those neural connections for regulating stress and when the basic lessons in understanding other minds were given, the relational environment was good-enough. But we need a mother's attentiveness and responsiveness as a sounding board for a sense of self long after infancy.

In the teen years, we are likely to have high-level demands for a parent's attention. Many of the common tensions between teen and parent occur as a son or daughter tries to update the parent: "This is who I am and what I think now. You see me as the child I used to be. But I've grown up, and I've changed." Teens are often excited by their ability to think independently, to reflect on political and moral principles, and to argue. They want to exercise their new powers on their parents. But Jenna describes a relationship with her mother that denies her this development. Her apparent maturity forecloses self-exploration. Jenna maintains a "good" relationship by giving priority to her mother's needs.

SNAPSHOT FOUR: YOUR HAPPINESS HURTS ME.

Rachel, age twenty-seven, is discouraged by her mother's responses to the good things in her life. A mother's delight in her child's independent interests, skills, and achievements is crucial to a good-enough relationship, in which a child feels that it is safe to develop her best possible self. Rachel feels betrayed when success and happiness expose her to rejection and ridicule. She marks a shift in her mother: when Rachel was a child her mother celebrated her growth; as she broached early womanhood—age sixteen—her independence and maturity attracted hostility. Rachel confronts a dilemma: she can pursue her goals and put her relationship with her mother at risk, or she can suppress her goals and maintain a "comfortable" relationship with her mother.

Once again, the dilemma is a choice between staying in relationship with herself and staying in relationship with her mother. Can she only preserve the apparent harmony of the relationship with her mother by changing, hiding, or denying who she really is?

SNAPSHOT FIVE: FAILURE TO SEE.

In this snapshot we see the young mother Sonia holding her seven-month-old son on her lap, with baby Kieran's head facing away, his eyes roaming the empty distance. When Kieran wriggles to a different position, Sonia holds him down and pins the baby's arms to his lap.

Seven-month-old Kieran has a baby's natural-born impulse to look at his mother, to track his mother's face, and to see his mother looking back at him. Normally this eye-to-eye engagement would enable a mother to pick up on her baby's rudimentary expression. A mother would develop and then demonstrate her understanding of the baby's cues. But Sonia ignores her baby's need for face-to-face contact. Sonia loves her baby and attends to his physical needs, but her failure to look at and learn from her child may create a lifelong struggle for Kieran. His expectations of human interaction are likely to be low. He may have trouble "reading" other people or expressing—even identifying—his own thoughts, feelings, and needs. He may be anxious and uncertain about close personal relationships and feel ambivalent about their value. A difficult mother at this early stage of life leads to lifelong difficulties.

Mentalization

"Trying to understand human nature is part of human nature," writes developmental psychologist Alison Gopnik. We spend a great deal of our waking (and dreaming) lives puzzling over the minds of other people. Why did she do that? Why did he speak to me like that? Are they telling the truth? Are they trying to trick me? Does he really like me or is he pretending? What are her motives?

There are good evolutionary reasons for our obsession with understanding other people. We are social creatures, dependent on one another for survival. The uniquely long period of a human's immaturity, where we remain dependent on parents for longer than any other species, has a lot to do with the need to learn about other people and, crucially, to grasp how people respond to us. To learn about other people, and also to learn about themselves, babies watch and consider and test other people's responses—and initially their greatest focus is on their mother. We need good teachers in this complex interpersonal world, and one way mothers teach children about their own inner states is by presenting their feelings back to the children. This important feedback allows us to acquire the crucial human skill called *mentalization*.

When a baby cries, distress and confusion fill his world. He is engrossed in the physical experience of discomfort. His entire body displays these overwhelming feelings. His chest heaves, his legs kick, his arms tense. When a mother responds, not by crying herself but with an expression of interest and concern, compos-ing her face in loving imitation of some features of distress—perhaps an exaggerated frown and a furrowed brow—she partly mirrors the baby's mental state but she also transforms it. She is able to make clear that by mirroring her baby's feelings she is not expressing her own feelings but looking into her child's.

This complex response is called *marked mirroring*. Doing simply what comes naturally to humans who care for babies, a mother engages in subtle and sophisticated communication. Her facial and vocal responses show that she shares her infant's feel-ings, not by having them herself, in the way the baby is experi-encing them, but by empathizing with them. She shows that she understands, and she also shows how to display understanding. The baby initially experiences distress in stark, physical terms. His mother re-presents his feelings to him—by showing con-cern, by selectively imitating him—and transforms his experi-ence into a concept about a mental state. Her understanding, attentiveness, acceptance, and concern are building blocks for his sense of self. She shows him that he has feelings and that he lives among other people who also have feelings and a men-tal life of their own. These separate people can connect with him and understand his inner states. He can mentalize—that is, reflect on his own thoughts and feelings and those of others—because his mother has shown him that his internal world has form and substance.

Mentalization and Emotional Intelligence

A mother's ability to learn about her baby's feelings and respond to her baby's cues is called *attunement*. No other animal brain is so dependent on this experience. As psychiatrist Thomas Lewis remarked, "The absence of attunement may be a non-event for a reptile, but it inflicts a shattering injury to the socially hungry, emotionally needy human infant." New findings in brain science show the biochemical impact of these early intense conversations. Brain circuits develop day by day that form the mental software for communication. The same experiences that structure these neural networks also shape the rudiments of what is now generally called emotional intelligence or the ability to manage, control, and identify our own emotions. Learning how to regulate our emotional states is now seen as the key task of infancy.

Our emotions can be terrifying when they are unregulated. We would be constantly flooded with anxiety, anger, and fear if we did not know how to comfort and reassure ourselves. We would be at the mercy of our impulses, unable to consider different ways of solving our problems and achieving our goals, if we could not identify and understand our emotions.

When we learn that going for a walk, eating chocolate, watching our favorite TV soap, or talking to a friend will help us calm down and regain our equilibrium after a disappointment or argument has set us awry, we are building on very early experiences. When we distinguish between the rational fear that leads us to be a careful driver and the irrational fear of ghosts, we are harnessing very early experiences of being startled and then soothed. Early experiences with a caregiver teach us how to get through an ordinary day without being overwhelmed by storms of fear, anxiety, or confusion.

Most of us can withstand the stress of changing circumstances and can test our immediate responses against past experience and accumulated understanding. Most of us can sense, understand, and react to the emotions of others—particularly people we are close to. None of us is born with these abilities. We acquire them, and our teacher is our primary caregiver. When she soothes us, holds us, and speaks softly to us, we experience the shift from feeling stress to feeling secure. When she shows us that she wants to learn about our feelings and sensations—what we need, why we are fussing—she introduces us to the positive stimulation of emotional exchanges with another person. These crucial early experiences form a good-enough environment whereby the brain controls the emotional floodgates. In short, our early interpersonal environment creates a buffer against the inevitable stresses awaiting us in our complex lives.

A baby who does not have this positive interactive stimulation can suffer as much harm as a baby who is subjected to physical abuse. The brain of a baby who is neglected, just like the brain of a baby who is abused, is infused with a different mix of biochemicals. This unhealthy mix of biochemicals prevents the growth of the neural circuits that buffer stress. Each setback, each hard knock reverberates with other negative experiences, and each experience of stress, disappointment, and frustration is overwhelming. A child deprived of positive interaction is less likely to learn healthy strategies for coping with difficult circumstances. Prolonged stress does not make you hardy; it actually makes you vulnerable. It reduces what the baby learns and it reduces the older child's ability to learn. Without the growth of those significant neural circuits in infancy, the brain loses its remarkable plasticity that normally offers the potential to absorb new skills throughout its lifespan.

We do not need a mother who is perfectly attuned to every thought and feeling; we need a good-enough mother who offers sufficient understanding for us to feel that our own experiences are real. Even when we have passed the brain-shaping stage of this powerful relationship, difficult, confusing, and threatening interactions with a mother can shake our sense of self.

Mirroring

We have seen how, to a child, his mother's face represents a mirror reflecting his inner states back to him. When she reflects a child's emotions, the mother marks this mirroring with playfulness, curiosity, and delight. The recognition and delight, the concern, fear, or disapproval displayed in a mother's face contains crucial information for the child: "This is the meaning of who I am and what I've done." When a mother's face expresses fear dismay, or disapproval, a child's own view shifts radically. A mother's response is seldom a matter of indifference to us. This process of looking to a mother to gauge the meaning of what we do continues even when we reach adulthood, but the meaning of her mirroring constantly changes.

As a child emerges from infancy and learns to move unaided, he or she tests the safety or danger of this new world by looking back to her mother's face to see her response. A child races away from her mother's side. The child's entire body is fired with plea-sure in her newfound motor abilities. As she turns to her mother she expects to see this joy reflected in her mother's face. She cries out in distress and loses her balance when instead she sees an expression of concern. As she falls, the physical jolt is only one cause of her screams; the real fear is triggered by the alarm in her mother's face.

A child delights in demonstrating her growing competence, but her joy can be shattered by a parent's disapproving or uneasy look. "Is it safe for me to move away from you?" and "Will I be able to find my way back?" and "Do my new abilities delight or distress you?" are some of the wide-ranging questions a child probes as she searches her mother's face. A child gets feedback about her character, her value, her abilities, her desires, and her goals from other family members. Grandparents, siblings, and cousins, friends, teachers, and neighbors reinforce and modify a child's sense of self, but the special importance of how a *mother* sees us begins in this early-mind-shaping relationship wherein a mother's response marks the meaning of what a child does.

As childhood draws to a close, the nature of a mother's mir-roring changes. Some children and many teens seem indifferent to a mother's approval or disapproval. But few adolescents, in spite of their bravado, actually cease to care what their mother thinks of them. They continue to watch her carefully and read her responses. They also try to shape her understanding and her judgment of them. Children are not passive receivers of their mother's responses. They work to shape what their mother sees and how she responds. As children grow, they engage in deliber-ate strategies for showing their mother how they have changed from the little child their mother thinks she knows. Teenagers see themselves as complex people, with independent and unexpected thoughts and feelings. Though having their own space and privacy may be increasingly important, they also want their parent to understand them, "see" them, and respect who they are.

Arguments between teenager and parent are often shaped by the teen's need to issue "identity reminders" as a means of teaching their parent how to be a better mirror. These reminders can come thick and fast, giving that characteristic edge to parent/teenager relationships. "I am not the child you think I am" and "I have new capabilities you haven't bothered to notice" are the implied messages that shape many parent/teen arguments.

These efforts are filled with pitfalls and frustrations. Teenagers may find that their mother is a slow learner who just doesn't see or understand what's in front of her. Complaints about a mother sometimes emerge from previous good-enough responses that set high expectations of her focuses and resonance. "She doesn't understand me" and "She doesn't listen" may arise from the very high standards she herself has set over the lifetime of the relationship. Arguments with our mother are often attempts to wrest from her that special attention and understanding that we continue to depend on, in some sense, long after her initial mirroring and re-presentation of our inner states have put their developmental stamp on our minds.

Teenagers' feistiness is often driven by the hope that their parent's understanding and appreciation will improve. Sons and daughters do not need a conflict-free relationship in order to thrive, but they need a dynamic and vital relationship, one that they can make sense of and influence. As they grow, as becoming their own person becomes a priority, they need a sounding board even for their most private thoughts and feelings. When a mother is slow to adjust to her child's changing sense of self, the teen complains because he wants to improve his mother's responses, the responses that remain so important to him. This ever-changing relationship rarely proceeds smoothly. Frustration and annoyance are inevitable. What damages a relationship is not roughness in the adjustment but being punished and scorned for trying to negotiate a more satisfactory relationship.

Making Sense

Our first lessons in life go beyond learning how to stay alive. They include learning that we communicate our feelings and needs to others. They include learning that significant caregivers provide an expressive repetoire of responses that help us understand ourselves. These early experiences form the template for knowing other people and being known by others. We want to be understood; we want assurance that we can communicate with others; but above all we expect that someone who cares for us will try to "know" us. She will look carefully, zoom in on what she sees, probe for further clues if she does not understand. We expect that someone so invested in our development will track and adjust to us as we grow. We trust that her deep engagement with us will be used to encourage and appreciate us rather than to control and criticize us.

Humans constantly try to make sense of other people's behavior. This is partly an evolutionary need to anticipate what other people will do, but it goes far beyond the need for physical survival. In a significant relationship we feel wrong-footed and constrained when someone repeatedly misconstrues and distorts our meanings, motives, and character.

In childhood, we thrive on our parent's delight in us and feel diminished by our parent's disapproval. In most cases, we make sense of our parent's different responses and learn what is acceptable and what is not. We also learn how to defend ourselves, explain our motives, and influence others' views of us. But when our parent claims to have full and fixed knowledge of who we should be and what we need to do, or when our parent's assessment of us is based primarily on her own needs, then we confront a terrible dilemma. We have to choose between valuing our own needs, developing our own thoughts, and identifying our own emotions, on the one hand, and maintaining a significant relationship with our parent, on the other.

A mother who imposes this dilemma is often unaware of the precise conditions she is setting. She may be overwhelmed by her own needs; her vision narrows and cuts off her child's perspective. When she was a child, she may have experienced prolonged stress from either neglect or abuse that has rendered her unable to manage her own emotions or respond to her child's. Her son or daughter may be the only person who "hears" her despair, and she may then come to depend on her child and see him or her as her caregiver. She may feel so powerless herself that she manipulates or terrifies or controls her child just to exercise some effect on her world.

Understanding a mother's difficulty does not ease the child's difficult experience. To a child the dilemma—"Either develop complex and constricting coping mechanisms to maintain a relationship with me, at great cost to your own outlook, imagination, and values, or suffer ridicule, disapproval, or rejection"—is a choice between life or death. During our early years, when our worlds are centered on the feelings and behavior of our parents, we need our mother's love and recognition as much as we need food and shelter. During those early years, our social brains are developing the patterns of expectation, interpretation, and emotional regulation that we carry forward into our adult lives. Older children, teenagers, and adults who are no longer strictly dependent on a mother may continue to think and feel and react according to the patterns established in the context of past vulnerabilities. They carry the difficult relational environment wherever they go. The legacy of a difficult mother is long-lasting. We can, however, learn to survive it, manage it, and in some cases benefit from it.

Chapter Three

THE ANGRY MOTHER

I. The Force of Anger

W HEN I was a child my mother's screams could take hold of my body. Though physical attacks—usually in the form of "well-deserved" spankings—were rare, her eyes worked their way into my skin, muscle, and bone. There was nothing left of me, no safe place for me when her anger was in full force. Long after it subsided and she was all smiles, I could feel its presence. It came to shape all aspects of my relationship with her.

My mother had a very different story about her anger. It was normal; it was exercised in the name of love. She saw it as a necessary expression of her parental duty. She explained that her exceptional anger arose from her exceptional standards of care.

If she shouted more than other mothers, it was because she knew more than most other people about what was right and what was wrong. She was teaching her child important lessons. She was not a "lazy" parent, as so many others were. Her explosive anger proved how much she cared.

I was not alone in suffering the force of her anger. Any outing to a store, any visit to a restaurant, any household repair job was likely to reveal to her some criminal act, and her duty was to call the perpetrator to account. She would leave the world a better place by ensuring that people did not "get away with things." She hoped that from her they would "know better next time." I could see that for the salesperson, waiter, or plumber she was "difficult"; but to them this difficulty was an episode that would end with the close of business. For me, her anger was written large on every page of every day.

My mother was not angry all the time. An objective account might show that eruptions in any given month could be counted on the fingers of one hand. These were for me, however, a matter of daily preoccupation. I constantly anticipated her anger, but I could never predict it. I began to play a game with myself: when I worried about some fault or failing—such as an imperfect grade on a school report, or a missed music lesson, or failure to return home "on the dot" of the agreed time—I would imagine her response in detail. I would "hear" her accusations and follow her words as they probed to the depths of my crime. I tried to control the outcome by imagining her anger. When I expected anger, there was indifference; when I anticipated approval, there was some action or word that would spark an explosion. On the grounds that I was likely to be wrong, I tried to use my pessimism as a talisman against the outcome I envisioned. I would imagine her anger in all its colorful glory; the more vivid my imagination, the more likely it would not become real. But this magical thinking (in reverse) only worked for actions and words I was able to spot as possible offenses. I had too many blind spots: I had not taken a helpful telephone message; I had forgotten to tell the electrician that something else needed repair; or perhaps the tone of my voice, the turn of my head, a particular phrase displayed some lack of "proper respect" and would fire up her smoldering anger.

I thought fury was an inevitable part of being a mother, and I was wary of becoming a mother myself. "You'll never appreciate your mother until you have children yourself," my mother used to say whenever I "whined." But when I had children myself, and witnessed their vulnerability, responsiveness, and exquisite sensitivity to their emotional environment, I was newly appalled by her behavior. My new appreciation was of the magnitude of her ruthlessness. This is not, I think, what she meant. I learned, too, that a three-year-old's irritability can strike your nerves at a pitch that reverberates with rage you didn't know you had. I discovered the sickly, shameful relief of bundling up all the day's frustrations and venting them at a child, watching her sweet face tense in fear and love while her arms reached out and up in a plea for reconciliation. And in *seeing* that response, I learned that there was a limit to my own infantile outbursts and that even the ugly, witch-like mother I modeled in my mind could be conquered—not once and for all, but by daily acts of responsiveness to a child's perspective. Nevertheless, I had gained the uncomfortable knowledge that a mean and difficult mother could reside in me, however much mother love I felt.

AS A PSYCHOLOGIST and as a mother, I am aware that all parents get angry. I am aware that, though no child likes it when a parent is angry, a single outburst does not produce a difficult relational environment. It is only when a parent repeatedly and regularly uses anger to close conversations, in the broadest sense of "conversation," that a dilemma is framed. When a parent uses anger or the threat of anger to dominate the emotional atmosphere, then even potentially good conversations with a parent lose spontaneity, openness, and honesty. When a parent's anger escalates in response to a son's or daughter's attempts to bring their own experience into the conversation, then the dilemma is framed: "Either restrict your behavior to suit me, or my anger will drive all comfort from the relationship." The condition then becomes: "Suffer my anger, respect my rage, if you want to remain close to me. If you challenge my right to inflict my anger on you, if you question the legitimacy of my rage, the relationship will become even more uncomfortable for you."

In this chapter I present case studies in which people describe their own experiences of this dilemma. These individual stories are analyzed in light of recent findings in neuroscience that explain why children respond so powerfully to a mother's anger. While these scientific findings mark possible negative consequences of a difficult relationship, they also suggest routes to recovery.

Imposing a Dilemma

"Everyone shouts," Lois protests, as she listens to her seventeen-year-old daughter Margot complain of "having to take a deep breath before I face Mom."

Margot appears to be voicing for the first time her own anger at having to constantly control herself in order to avoid her mother's outbursts. Her eyes are bright with alarm at her own courage. She flicks the fleshy pad of her thumbs up and down against the short, bitten nails on her index and ring fingers.

"Mom's voice gets so loud, it's like it's splitting your head in two, and I have to concentrate hard. Like I'm running alongside that fast-flowing anger, and if I can only keep up I can stop it from flooding me. I freeze inside and wait for it to pass. But the next thing I know, she's shouting at me for not paying attention while she's shouting."

Lois tosses her head. "So, I have a short fuse. Since when does shouting kill you? She's the one who makes me shout. If she respected my wishes, I wouldn't shout. She makes life difficult for herself, but she knows I love her anyway."

Most children do their utmost to resist a difficult mother's dilemma until, after repeated frustrations, they learn that their efforts will only result in punishment. A child wants her mother to see things from her point of view: "This is what your anger feels like to me." An angry mother, however, will respond with further accusations. She justifies her own behavior, discounts her child's experience, and blames her child for their own suffering. Within seconds, the "conversation" closes. The child's resistance becomes fuel to feed the mother's anger.

Love and Rejection: A Classic Double Bind

A difficult relational dilemma is hedged with contradictions that can be described as a double bind. A classic example of the double bind is a declaration of love in a context of negative cues such as tone of voice or body language. When a mother expresses disgust or hostility and insists she is expressing love, a child is trapped between two messages: fear and safety. The implication is that there is no difference between the two.

Fear drives a child to observe a mother closely. The smallest pull in a mother's mouth, any constriction in her eyes, any tension in her neck signals danger. When the words spoken do not match the language of face and voice and body, the child ceases to make sense of the relational world.

Mother love is a loaded topic. It wears a sacred mantle and is protected from criticism. Sometimes calling up maternal love clouds the issue someone is trying to understand. "I'm your mother and I love you" may convey the message "I am giving you everything you want, and you are wrong to want more." "I am your mother and I love you," calls up cultural icons that bear the message, "I have this magical store of maternal love, and therefore you are ungrateful and ungenerous if you complain about me."

Sometimes a difficult mother is defined as a mother unable to love her children, but difficult mothers often feel love and genuinely see themselves as acting in the name of love. A buzz-word for the type of love a mother ought to have for a child is "unconditional love." An idealized version of unconditional love means, "I love you totally and accept you fully and do not judge you, ever." But this does not fit the passionate responsibility parents feel for a child. Good-enough parents set conditions they expect a child to meet. They scold and advise and direct, and they have strong views, sometimes negative, about a child's words and actions and preferences and values. "I love you unconditionally," simply means, "Whatever the circumstances, I won't abandon you." But without a relationship in which feelings are shared and understanding is offered, a child is likely to feel frozen out of her mother's love, even when she says, "I love you."

Difficult Routines

It takes many years of careful observation and reflection before a son or daughter can articulate the terms of a relational dilemma. When you are embedded in a difficult relationship you are subject to tactics that coerce you to comply with its terms; simultaneously the mother who coerces you denies the existence of a dilemma. When a child struggles to resolve or confront or escape the dilemma, a difficult mother is likely to maintain the status quo through a number of different strategies.

Normally, children have their parents' help in developing their powers of reflection and control, but parents who foster a difficult relationship are unlikely to be reflective themselves. Sometimes they deny that they are angry even when they are shouting. They are often unable to stand back and consider whether they are justified in being angry. They view a child's distress as "silly" or "naughty" or "spoiled." In spite of their failure to reflect on their own emotions and behavior, however, they often display considerable intelligence in their ability to confuse and oppose a child. Here are some of the routines frequently used to prevent a child from seeing where the difficulties lie:

Incoherence in some form sits at the heart of most difficult relationships. A child's suffering is compounded by a parent's refusal to acknowledge that suffering. Nor can a child get a parent's help in understanding what their anger is about. Uncontrolled anger tends to be self-justifying. Blame sticks to it like glue, so that everything that pops into the angry parent's mind is the fault of the child and everything the parent has ever been angry about is swept up in the whirlwind of her present fury. The only sense a child can make of this is, "I am utterly in the wrong, and I have no ability to understand my interpersonal world."

Marginalization, or dismissing the significance of a child's protest. Marginalization is a version of denial. It signals, "You do not feel what you say you feel." Hearing this from a parent is self-alienating. The message is, "I don't know what I feel" and "I am not in a position to name my own feelings."

Counteraccusation shifts a child's complaint about a parent to the child herself. The message is, "It is your fault that you are suffering." Often, counteraccusation comes in two parts. The first part is the message that the child deserves a parent's anger. The second part is the message that the child is wrong to object to a parent's anger because it is for the child's own good.

Obfuscation screens over the issue that a child tries to raise. If a child protests that his mother's anger distresses him, she may insist, "I love you, so I am really giving you all you need." The powerful term "love" draws a curtain over the complex and urgent feelings the child tries to convey. Obfuscation often works alongside marginalization to underline the message, "Your suffering is not real."

Narrow vision means that someone cannot—or is not willing—to see something from another's point of view. "My way of looking at things is the only legitimate way of looking at things" is the underlying message. A consequence of narrow vision is that a parent feels fully justified in refusing to consider whether her anger is warranted.

Externalizing is a way for a parent to admit that her behavior is at fault while ensuring that she remains innocent. "It's the booze, not me" is an excuse that directs a child to dissociate her experience of her mother from her "real" mother.

Accusation via mindreading involves an angry parent projecting her own dark expectations onto a child. She may justify her anger by saying, "I know what you're thinking" and "I know what you want." The parent then ceases to listen (in a broad sense) to a child, because listening isn't necessary. It is deeply confusing for a child to be told that her mother can know her without listening or attending to her. The implication is that the child's mind is not his own.

Combination tactics use several or even all of these maneuvers to confuse a child and defeat argument. Combination tactics generate such volatility and incoherence that a child is likely to give up his protest and agree to the terms of the difficult dilemma.

II. The Science of Fear

MANY PEOPLE say that they do not know why they panic in the face of a mother's anger. Even in adulthood they may feel a primitive terror. Here, Craig, age twenty-one, and Robert, age thirty-four, reflect on the nature of their fear.

Craig says:

I know she's not going to kill me, but on some level I'm not sure I really do know that. When she's angry with me I feel I'm up against a firing squad.

Robert reflects:

I go weak at the knees when she turns against me. I forget what it's like to feel courage. I try to remind myself that the worst of it will pass, that she won't be like that forever. She's mad now, but there will come a time when she's not mad. When I was growing up, I tried all sorts of things to get me through these times. I used to think, "It won't be so bad if she doesn't hit me." And then I got to noticing that whether she hit me or didn't hit me didn't much matter. What I was really afraid of was that she was going to explode and disappear.

These profound fears are embedded in childhood dependence. A parent's anger is a signal of danger. A child who sees a parent in the grip of uncontrolled anger fears for himself but also fears for the parent. The child's unconscious terror is not only that he'll be harmed but also that the anger will consume his mother. A child's response can roughly be described as, "My mother is out of control, so I have no one to protect me." This state of terror is similar to what any young primate experiences when it is physically abandoned by its mother.

"SHOUTING DOESN'T KILL YOU" may be literally true, but at certain times in a child's life a parent's anger can cause great developmental harm.

We are not born with the brain circuitry that allows us to understand and regulate our emotions. Nevertheless, we are fully capable of *feeling*. In fact, because early fear is experienced without any system for putting feelings into context, there are no brakes, no boundaries to the power of those early primitive feelings. Vulnerable and raw, very young children are easily overwhelmed by fear.

Primitive mental circuits associate a mother's anger with danger, both internal and external. This alarm is signaled by the part of the brain called the amygdala. The amygdala is a cluster of linked structures shaped like two almonds. They sit near the bottom of the limbic areas of the brain; these are the source of passionate feelings, including pleasure and desire as well as fear. One of the central roles of the amygdala is to trigger the biochemical cascade of the flight-or-fight response. In short, the amygdala ensures our rapid response to danger.

This mental alarm system does a lot to protect us. Before we can consciously assess a situation and identify the cause of alarm, we feel fear physically in our bodies. This fast-system helps a competent human survive, but it can be toxic to the young, developing brain. When the infant's brain is flooded repeatedly with fear, the growth of those receptors and connections necessary to identify and understand feelings is stalled. The more young children experience fear, the less well equipped their brains are for absorbing shocks.

How the Brain Learns About Emotion Management

Increasingly, neuroscientists and psychologists are focusing on the significance that emotion plays in the organization and creation of a child's self. During infancy and very early childhood, the right brain—the neurological location of the emotional self—holds the key to healthy development. The right brain is activated for processing emotional information, interpreting faces, and assessing new and unusual situations. Key to this brain development is a close relationship with another person, almost always a mother. A mother provides a healthy social and emotional environment through her capacity to monitor and regulate her own emotions—especially negative emotions such as anger—because to develop strong neural systems, a child needs to be protected from prolonged and intense stress.

Of course all babies experience distress, but in a good-enough relationship they develop skills to withstand mood changes and to adapt to the changing world. A responsive parent sees that her baby is uncomfortable, tired, cold, hungry, or in pain; she then soothes and comforts him, adjusting her voice and gestures to her infant's emotional rhythms. She shows that she and her child can work together to recapture comfort, safety, and the delight of human interaction. As the child engages in what is called an "affective dialogue" or emotional exchange, he is able to build a model for emotion and mood management.

The feelings aroused by the sights, sounds, smells, and touch of an attentive mother are burned into the developing limbic circuits of the brain. The ebb and flow of emotion promotes experience vital to resilience. Gradually a child learns not to get too upset about one thing, because one bout of stress is not the end of the world. Gradually he learns that his attention can be deflected from pain back to something enjoyable. In time he learns to stem his flood of anxiety, to find effective ways to relax, to discharge negative feelings, to appreciate and enjoy his environment.

These interactions that teach a child to regulate his own feelings produce a pattern of experiences called "rupture and repair." When a child is able to experience over and over again the transition from negative to positive emotion, his young brain is stimulated to build circuits and systems for emotional regulation. While these circuits and systems are forming, a child "borrows" a parent's self-control.

How a Stressful Environment Impedes Emotion Management

Throughout childhood and adolescence, the social brain systems used to gain insight into emotions and thoughts—our own and those of others—develop more slowly when the brain is constantly flooded with stress chemicals. Imagine then the physiological disadvantage of a child whose mother cannot positively reflect his emotions or manage her own.

In some families, outbursts and grumpiness are normal. A continuous "nattering"—scolding, complaining, whining, mocking, and rebuking—can be heard. Everything a child does, however harmless, becomes a target for complaint or accusation. In such circumstances, where bad temper is the norm, anger has to be revved up a notch every time it wants to rise above the usual level of carping. The more anger there is in a family, the more likely it is that anger will escalate. In these circumstances, the constant stress impedes a child's ability to understand, to reflect, and to regulate his or her own emotions.

In such an environment, children have trouble processing signals from other people. They are quick to anticipate danger with any shift in facial expressions and gestures. They may respond aggressively or defensively in situations that most people would handle easily. Without the ability to regulate their own emotions, they may swing between fear, anguish, and pain, then to a sense of inexplicable calm, only to lurch again into an overwhelming sense of danger. Though there are many routes to learning and many opportunities to learn what we may have missed earlier, learning itself becomes more difficult when prolonged childhood stress reduces the brain's plasticity. When subjected to prolonged stress, the brain actually has less capacity to grow, learn, and adapt to new ways of coping. So those children who have the greatest need to develop new ways of reflecting on and managing their inner lives are likely to be the least able to do so.

Raw Experiences of a Parent's Anger

Here are the voices of three young people in search of their own guidelines for managing panic and distress. They describe the overwhelming physical response and their urgent search for some place of safety.

Nine-year-old Sam feels "a rock in my stomach" when his mother shouts. "I have to sit real still, otherwise my stomach's gonna rip apart. I bend over and sit real still." He waits until there's a break in the shouting, and then, when he thinks it is safe to sit upright, "I imagine banging all the bad stuff into the rock, and then burying the rock so it's put away. When I do this I can get on with things because I don't have to carry it around anymore."

Sandy, age eleven, says, "I get a huge lump in my throat when Mom is mad. It's as hard as a stone. I can't swallow. I can't talk. It's worse than the worst sore throat I've ever had." Sandy pictures coating it with "the best ice cream ever" and imagines the rich sweetness slipping down and filling her with pleasure. "When I see my mom's about to get really angry and start in on me, I can look forward to thinking about the ice cream. Sometimes my throat eases enough for me to speak up, and I don't even sound sad, and I should practice that because that seems to calm Mom down. I think about things I might say and things she might say. I don't know, sometimes if she sees I'm sad, she switches from mean to nice, but sometimes it helps if I don't cry because she can get mad at me for crying."

Before she falls asleep at night, Sandy likes to "file things in boxes, and when they are horrible, I squish the file closed, and you can't get it, even with a password. I don't tell anyone about them. I don't tell my best friend. I don't even tell my kitten. The good things I try to have passwords for so I can remember them."

Laura, age thirteen, says, "My mother is like a hurricane when she's angry. Everything that gets in her path is destroyed. While she's in full force I try to think about what to say. I feel so angry myself. I want to explode in her face. And sometimes I do. Or I go in my room and slam the door. And I keep imagining things I could say or do to stop her dead. Anything, from kicking her and punching her, to saying just the right words that make her shut up. I get these scenes in my head and play them over and over again."

A PARENT'S ANGER may not kill a child, but children experience its force as a physical assault. These children try to teach themselves basic strategies to manage their emotions without an internal model of a parent who contains her own. They try to assemble their own tool kit for managing their difficult environment. Their awkward and cumbersome efforts absorb massive mental energy.

How Children Try to Manage Fear

When a family environment produces prolonged stress, children seek ways of soothing themselves. They are at a disadvantage because they do not have a parent's emotional management to model, so they seek other means to manage fear.

Repetition Compulsion

One common method of fear management is a version of what Freud called *repetition compulsion*. We keep repeating an experience in an attempt to reduce the anxiety associated with it.

Freud observed his grandson throwing a toy out of his crib and then showing distress as he gazed longingly at the distant toy. But this toy was attached to a string, and the child was able to pull it toward him and retrieve it through the bars of the crib. When he grasped it, he shivered with delight, but he immediately threw it out again, and again he showed great distress as he gazed at the distant toy. The child was absorbed in this game for long stretches of time. When he threw the toy out of the crib, he said, "Gone," and when he reeled it back in and grasped it, he said, "Here."

Freud realized that the child was reenacting his mother's comings and goings. The game put the child in control of his mother's movements. But, Freud wondered, if the purpose of the game was to enjoy the fantasy of being in control, then why did the child not simply keep the toy close to him, as he wanted to keep his mother close to him?

Eventually, Freud concluded that the game served another crucial purpose. By repeating the experience of a mother being "gone" and being "here," the child was trying to overcome the anxiety associated with his mother's comings and goings. We sometimes mentally play out over and over unpleasant experiences in order to reduce the power of the feelings associated with them—a process Freud called "mastery."

The compulsion to repeat uneasy experiences may be intended to reduce anxiety, but it can have a very different effect. A child who pours energy into imagining a mother's anger may end up internalizing that angry voice. This then forms a neuro-linguistic program that saps the child's energy and confidence. "You deserve to be disappointed" and "You always mess up" become automatic responses to every negative experience. Instead of reducing the effect of the mother's anger, they inflict continuous self-punishment.

Trying to Improve the Script

Another way a child may try to manage her fear is to plot scenarios in which she scripts ways to placate or distract a mother.

Based on repeated exposure to a mother's outbursts, some children imagine different things they might say or do to moderate their mother's anger. They focus on past arguments, or envision possible arguments, and mull them over line by line, wondering how they might change the dramatic flow. If I say this, will I get her attention? If I avoid saying that, will her anger lie dormant? If I keep cool, will her anger die down? If I cry, will she feel bad?

As children mentally relive angry scenarios, they may get a clearer picture of what is going on. They may succeed in identifying a reasonable management strategy, but there is also the likelihood that these scenarios will not reduce their emotional disturbance. Instead, they overstimulate their own anger and outrage. Far from regulating their emotions, they are whipping them into a storm.

Stonewalling

Some children try to close themselves to all feeling rather than experience pain, as Sam does with his "rock." *Stonewalling* is the technique of shutting down receptors and turning your body and mind into a stone wall. This can be a defense against the stimuli that flood our system when we sense danger. Sam closes down all circuits and sits in the classic "crash" position we are instructed to take in the event of an air crash. Both Sam and Laura brace themselves to avoid being overwhelmed by their own emotions. Sandy, with her file boxes, tries to lock her experiences away and keep them out of her daily life with her friends. This strategy reduces anxiety, but at the price of freezing all feeling.

Acceptance

Some children conclude that a parent's anger is justified. It can be more painful to believe that a parent is uncontrolled, unreasonable, and spiteful than to see yourself at fault. It can be more painful to look on confusion and chaos than to make sense of a parent's behavior by concluding that you deserve her punishment. This experience is powerfully described by Diane Rehm in her autobiography *Finding My Voice*. When her mother beat her, she kept the beating a secret because she believed that she deserved to be beaten when she disappointed her parents. Her mother's anger, and her mother's way of expressing that anger, became the daughter's secret shame.

Trying to make sense of other people's responses to us is a basic human activity. Accepting a mother's anger by concluding that it is justified is a way of making sense of a difficult relationship. But this acceptance comes at a great cost, for it means that we see their cruelty as our shame.

Internalizing Anger

A consequence of either repetition compulsion or acceptance may be internalization of the mother's angry voice. Hearing her anger played and replayed in your own head blurs the distinction between her anger and your own thoughts.

Most children hear their mother's voice over and over again in their mind's ear. Usually that internalized voice is soothing and comforting. The words we imagine, which first made their impact in that foundational relationship, help us weather disappointment or assuage unease. "Things will be okay" and "You did your best," or "You didn't mean to do that; it was an accident," are ancient tropes we tell ourselves to reduce anxiety. Children who internalize a mother's angry voice speak different words that inflict punishment, even when they are outside the reach of the actual mother's anger. In the next section we look at case studies of adults who continue to do battle with their lingering fear.

III. The Legacy of Anger

PSYCHOLOGISTS RECOGNIZE that cumulative frightening experiences leave their mark as "a secret inscription, a frozen image, or template." A mother may see her angry outbursts as temporary and inconsequential, but to a son or daughter they color the entire world. High-functioning, independent adults continue to carry this secret inscription within them. Sensitivity to a parent's anger begins with an infant's dependence and love, but it does not end there.

"No matter how old I get," Steve, age thirty-six, reflects, "when she shouts I might as well be three years old again. I feel trapped and utterly at her mercy. Once I hear that angry voice, up pops that little guy who's totally dependent and can't do a thing for himself. I pretty much feel I can't be anything when she's mad at me."

Audrey, now forty-one, describes her life with her mother as "living on an emotional roller coaster. She is often calm, even laid back. Then the world changed and it would be a fearful place, where everything made her angry." She remembers the "terror of her yells reeling across the kitchen," the "knife-like darts" of her eyes, the "mean set of her mouth."

At age forty-seven, Gabriel reflects, "I could never predict what would spark my mother's anger. But when she was angry, I had no power. I couldn't say anything without making things worse."

At the age of thirty-eight, Robert feels no better equipped than a child to change the system of interaction. He says, "I stand there, waiting for the anger to burn out, feeling helpless as a baby."

Emotions and Memory and the Impact of Fear

The term "implosion" was used by the psychoanalyst Ronald Laing to describe a person's sense that their whole world is about to crash in on them or implode. We are vulnerable to implosion when we feel we have no inner defenses. A mother's anger can take us back to those early experiences, when we ourselves had no brain circuits for bringing us back to an emotional equilibrium and instead had to "borrow" or depend on hers. When we see our mother lose control over her emotions, memories of our own helplessness are triggered.

Early dependence creates a powerful memory context. Once a strong emotion has been imprinted on the fast-response system of the brain, it can be triggered again by anything associated with the original fear. Even when the child's dependence is long past, the adult can experience anxiety very much like that of a helpless infant.

Childhood memories have a special vividness. Before our brain develops "schema" or general concepts of the things we see everyday—such as tables and trees and toys—we pay exquisite attention to details. Before schema process observations with speed and efficiency, the particularity of individual things stands out. This underlies the richness of childhood memories, which are processed before the mind learns to take shortcuts to the gist of a place, person, or action. Children who experience a difficult emotional environment may lack such vivid childhood memories. For them, childhood memories may be vague or patchy because their energy has been deployed defensively.

An angry mother may inflict specific traumas, such as physical assault, or may generate long-term low-grade anxiety. Whether stress results from one awful event or a persistent uncomfortable emotional climate, it can damage the hippocampus—the brain's memory storage facility. When this part of the brain is damaged, explicit memories—the words actually spoken, the incident that gave rise to the argument, even details about who hit whom and when—cannot be put in context, analyzed, or understood. The child retains a strong emotional reaction to sensations, impressions, sounds, sights, or smells that are associated with the stressful events, but he lacks a broader understanding of what happened and why. For example, a child may have no conscious memory of being locked for hours in a cupboard, yet anything that is in some way associated with such a place—whether it is a musty scent, darkness, or the click of a latch—sparks strong feelings of fear. A child may not have a specific memory of being hit, but a gesture or voice that for any reason is associated with the attack triggers panic. In such cases, physical fear is aroused in the amygdala—those deep-brain almond-shaped nuggets in which our fast-responses such as fear are processed—but the damage to the hippocampus, where memories and their contexts are stored, means that there is no *conscious* memory of the event that made the child afraid.

Throughout childhood—and often beyond—a parent's anger is experienced as a primitive threat. The fast-system in the brain triggers early experiences of helplessness, and we respond as we would in a real crisis of danger. If we are lucky, our slower analytic brain systems remember that this anger is limited to a specific context, and we expect calm and contentment when the anger subsides. When a child learns that a mother is normally in control of her feelings, it is easier to accept the ups and downs of daily life. The child's brain is rich with receptors for stress chemicals, and he can roll with the punches. But when we live with a mother who cannot regulate her feelings, the long-term anxiety disrupts our own emotion management, and panic can be triggered by any number of internal and external cues. In many ways it is like watching a horror film, when you expect a terrifying figure to leap out at you, but its sudden appearance nonetheless jolts you out of your seat.

In order to defuse the primitive fear and stem the panic we can barely explain, we need to understand the context in which our fear occurred. People who have specific, detailed memories of the chaotic storms of their childhood are more likely to be resilient and overcome the brain's physiological disadvantage. We have a better chance of seeing the limitations of a bad experience if we can see that a frightening event occurred in the past and that it will not necessarily recur repeatedly. If implicit memories can be made explicit, they can be freed from the tyranny of fast-response fears.

Auditing the Effects of Parental Anger

As we try to understand what effect a difficult mother may have had on us, we need to look back to past experiences and try to "hold our mind in mind." This simply means that we notice and reflect on previously unexamined responses and memories.

Begin by describing your reactions to your mother's anger, whether in the past or in the present.

Are you fearful?
- If so, can you explore this fear?
- What is the worst result you can imagine?

- Is it realistic to feel that her anger might kill you?
- Is it realistic to suppose that you won't be able to function if she remains angry?
- Are you worried that *she* will die from her own excess of anger?

In allowing yourself to focus on your fears, you can test them.

Are your fears realistic?
- Can you modify your response so that it is realistic?

    Perhaps, on reflection, you realize that the worst imaginable outcome is that she will continue to shout and that she will remain angry.

    Perhaps you know from experience that though her anger sometimes escalates into physical violence, you can leave the room and protect yourself.
- Can you reflect on the number of times you have survived her anger?

    Haven't you experienced the end to her and your painful feelings many times before?
- Can you use these reminders as reassurance that you can survive this time, too?

Then take a look at your current feelings toward her.

- Are you angry at her?
- Do you blame yourself for "making" her angry?
- Can you consider whether this blame serves any purpose? (For example, does it protect her from your anger?)
- Do you continue to worry about or monitor her anger?

- Do you think that by holding her anger in your mind, you will be able to control it?
- Do you find yourself speaking to yourself in her angry voice?

The purpose of posing these questions is to consider whether you are wasting energy trying to control your mother's anger when your energy would be more efficiently directed to regulating your own responses to her anger.

If you hear her angry words in your thoughts whenever something in your life goes awry, then write the words down. When you read what you've written, it is likely that you will see how excessive your self-directed anger is. You may read something like, "That was a stupid thing to say, and you're always stupid, and everyone who heard you thinks you are worthless. Now you'll lose your job, and your friends will also see that you are worthless, and you'll never have any friends again." It is likely that seeing your thoughts in black and white will make them more amusing than threatening.

NEXT, CONSIDER THREE common outcomes of adapting to an angry mother, and consider whether any of these apply to you.

The Appeaser

Some people who have adapted to an unpredictable and angry relationship with a mother assume a sweet, ingratiating persona. They hope to appease the rage they see beneath every greeting and smile. Personal interactions tend to be geared to pleasing and placating others rather than to genuine engagement.

If you are an appeaser, you may feel a surge of anxiety at any outburst (or even a hint) of anger in others. You rush forward to placate them. You may assume that others are behaving appropriately in expressing anger toward you. In some cases, you may even be attracted to people whose anger is easily aroused because you associate that behavior with attachment and authority.

TO ASSESS WHETHER you adopt this strategy, ask yourself to describe the partners and friends you choose and what qualities you find attractive.

- Do you find something comforting about being shouted at?
- Do you feel ashamed when someone expresses anger toward you?
- Do you follow other people's moods obsessively?
- Is maintaining others' composure a priority in your interactions with them?

IN CONDUCTING THIS emotional audit, you may find that being an appeaser is indeed a legacy of a difficult relational environment, but you may consider it a skill. Perhaps you are the company diplomat. Perhaps everyone wants you at parties to deal with their difficult friends and relatives. But you may want more control over when you are diplomatic and when you are direct. You might want to have the confidence that you have the option to be assertive on certain occasions. You might want to put less energy into placating others and more into genuine interactions.

In conducting this emotional audit, you might find that, yes, your partner tends to shout easily, but the shouting contains no malice and passes quickly. Perhaps your partner's short fuse does not prevent him or her from being loving and supportive. In that case, you may have found a gem whom others have avoided because they cannot get past the bursts of temper. But if you find that, time after time, a partner or close friend disappoints you by being "just like" a difficult parent, then you would do well to consider whether you are selecting someone who helps you reproduce that difficult relationship.

If you realize that you blame yourself and feel ashamed when someone is angry at you, then you might step back and take another look and consider the motives for a person's anger and how their lack of emotional control might be someone else's problem, not yours.

The Stonewaller

Some people who have adapted to unpredictable anger in a relationship tend to stonewall whenever they pick up any hint of anger in another person. Going blank, refusing to show a response, leaving the room, are all defensive acts of a stonewaller.

We turn into a stone wall because we fear that anything we do will escalate the threat. Or we may try to be "hard" so as not to be hurt and alarmed by another's anger.

Withdrawing from the heat of an argument may prevent us from being attacked and may prevent us from responding aggressively, but it tends to infuriate others. They may be trying to engage with you when they argue. If you respond by shutting down, you may be responding to past experiences rather than to the present one. Perhaps you think that every heated response will result in the explosions you previously experienced from your mother.

Some people are able to make a clear distinction between their past fear of a mother's anger and their present-day responses to others' anger. But if you close down in response to any heated emotion, and you assume that strong feeling is tantamount to being out of control or hysterical, then you may be impeded by a fast-fear response.

NOTICE YOUR INITIAL responses to the emotional cues you pick up. Can you stop to consider whether another person's display of feeling is really the beginning of a terrible emotional explosion? Do you perhaps jump to the conclusion that someone is angry? Can you try waiting to see what develops? Can you regulate your physiological arousal—the increased heart rate, the rush of adrenaline—to withstand a heated exchange and find some way other than stonewalling or shutting down and making yourself into an unresponsive "wall"?

Try to identify the worst thing that might happen if you remain engaged with someone who is angry. When you have gone through possible outcomes (for example, "he'll shout at me," "he'll glare," "he'll call me names"), consider how you might deal with it. You may find that your expectations are unfounded. This should give you confidence to remain engaged in the future. Or, if you find that there are negative repercussions, you may find that you can handle them after all.

The Replicator

Psychologists have long noticed that people have a tendency to repeat patterns of behavior they have seen in their parents. Sometimes they simply model a parent's behavior, but there are far more subtle and intractible patterns of repetition that can bind us to our pasts even as we think we are taking steps to escape.

Perhaps you think that your most pressing goal is to escape your mother's abuse. However, you may seek out a partner who psychologically resembles your mother and find that you have walked right back into a difficult relationship. Perhaps you choose to be close to someone who turns out to be as volatile as your mother and who inflicts discomfort all too familiar to you. Or perhaps gradually, over time, your partner or a close friend becomes like your mother; that may be because you unconsciously behave in ways that encourage others to treat you as your mother did.

One problem is that when we have a difficult parent, some behavior seems normal, and we fail to be alerted to words, actions, and gestures that would raise alarm bells in someone who is accustomed to more comfortable relationships. Sometimes we feel unsafe if we do not carry these familiar patterns of abuse around with us.

Sometimes our implicit memories of a parent's behavior lead us to repeat behavior even when it was painful. Rachel says, "I don't want to be like my mother," but when she becomes a mother herself, the familiar words and tone and responses come alive.

TO ASSESS WHETHER you are at risk of replicating the model of an angry parent, ask yourself the following:

- Do I frequently hear an inner voice berating me even for very minor mistakes?
- When I let off steam, even for a short period, do I worry that I have ruined everything?

- When I get angry, do I feel that I speak with someone else's voice?

If you fear that losing your temper, even for a moment, is destructive, you may be confusing ordinary temper loss with a very different kind of anger. Observe the effect of your anger on the people around you, particularly your children. If their discomfort is short-lived, if you are soon able to get back to a comfortable relational routine, then you should allow yourself to forget your outburst, just as they have. Children, after all, are built to withstand normal mood fluctuations.

If, when you are angry, you feel "possessed" by uncontrollable feelings and by someone else's voice, if you are appalled by the vehement and cruel words that come out of your mouth, if you ever engage in physical violence, then you may benefit from professional intervention tailored to your needs. You may be repeating a pattern that is deeply ingrained and require guidance in learning new positive patterns of managing stress.

Why Understanding Helps

Prolonged and frequent exposure to a parent's angry outbursts casts a long shadow. Sons and daughters who describe a parent's anger as unpredictable feel constantly wrong-footed and constrained; yet they also feel angry themselves and wish their anger had the power to do damage.

Mothers have no prerogative on anger. A father, grandfather, or stepfather can also terrorize a child who then lives in constant anticipation and dread of the next explosion. Many people other than a mother can create a difficult relational environment; but our intimate history in which we first conceptualized our inner lives through our mother's responses leaves most of us with a particular sensitivity and vulnerability to a mother's anger, whatever our age and whatever our status in the wider world. When we understand this context, we have a better shot at managing the impacts of our emotional history.

Chapter Four

THE CONTROLLING MOTHER

I HAVE SEEN young children, teenagers, and even adults shake and weep with frustration as they come up against a mother's assurance that she is the expert on their needs, wishes, and goals. This "expert" knowledge justifies her control. A child who is deprived of trust and interest in his or her own experiences feels confused, angry, and betrayed.

I recall such feelings when I was a child. Pressed hard against my mother's iron will, I braced myself against the waves of frustration that rocked my world but to which she was impervious. "Hah!" she exclaimed as she coolly observed my fury. "You'd be sorry if I listened to you. Do you really think you want me to be like those other mothers, who let their children do just as they please?"

I could not answer that question as a child. Nor is it easy to answer it now. What, after all, is the difference between being firm and being controlling?

When I tell my fourteen-year-old daughter, "No, you can't go out tonight. You have homework, you have school tomorrow, and you were out last night," am I exerting reasonable parental control or am I being controlling? When my daughter complains that she will miss an important shared experience with her friends and that she can easily finish her homework during a free study period in the morning, and I still say no, am I being firm or controlling?

Isn't a parent supposed to be strong and sure? Isn't it important to teach a child that there are some things that cannot be negotiated? A child has to be taught that some behavior simply cannot be tolerated. An impulsive teenager benefits when a parent controls him until he learns self-control. Control surely is an essential part of a good parent's job, not an attribute of a difficult parent?

Considering, weighing, assessing where a child requires control and where a child requires freedom is one of the most difficult balancing acts parents have to perform. Children complain that a parent's control is unreasonable even when it protects and guides them. Children's desires and impulses, if uncontrolled, would put them at grave risk. Teenagers complain that a parent controls them "like a child" or "ruins their life" by being controlling, when that is precisely what a parent is trying to avoid. The key to distinguishing positive control from being "controlling" is to assess the context. Do the regulations or expectations imposed allow for change over time as a child develops? What are the means by which control is imposed? Is it fairly reasoned? Are the explanations coherent? Or are orders fired like bullets in a relentless battle against a child's "willfulness"? Is control imposed with threats of dire consequences? Is control imposed with contempt for a child's own needs and goals? Is a child's own judgment mocked—for example, with "You think you're just so smart" and "Who do you think you are?" Does a parent constantly undercut a child's own views, perhaps with reminders of her superior experience—for example, "I've seen more of life than you" and "I've seen you make one mistake after another." Or perhaps control is imposed with a show of kindness, whereby a child is seen to be in constant need of a parent's input. But excessive control, even when imposed tenderly, carries the message, "You cannot be trusted to make your own decisions."

In essence, a controlling parent sees a child's individual will as something that should be broken. A firm parent, on the other hand, wants to protect and guide a child's will, leaving it intact.

Using Fear to Control

Parents are responsible for their children's safety and well-being. Their job is to teach their children that certain behaviors are harmful. When a mother shouts, "Don't touch that! You'll burn yourself," as a child reaches for a casserole dish just out of the oven, she may make her child cry but she imparts an important lesson. However, these necessary lessons can be misused. In my research on mothers and teenagers, I came to understand that threats often are used to bypass reasonable control. Susie, age sixteen, asks her mother whether she can go out, and her mother, Tammy, demands, "What do you mean? Go out on the street? Now? It's dark. Do you want to be attacked?"

Many parents resort to shortcuts in the heat of the moment, issuing commands without providing any explanation, when they have worn themselves out trying to impart wisdom and logic, or when they are simply tired, out of time, or at the end of their tether. But when threats become routine, when they form the primary mode of argument between parent and child, then coercion can seep into the very structure of a relationship. These routine threats have a three-pronged message. First, they contain dire predictions: "You'll be sorry" and "You'll pay for this" and "You don't know what you're in for." Second, they make the unreasonable claim that a parent's control is necessary to the child's well-being. When a third part of the message is that a child's own wishes and desires are inevitably dangerous and bad, then practice and moral guidance are transformed into a kind of witchcraft. Contempt is poured like molten rock onto a child's inner states, and the child becomes terrified of his or her own inner states. The son or daughter then faces a dilemma: Do I resist my parent's control and expose myself to the dangers of my own feelings, or do I succumb to my parent's control and give up my own desires and goals?

Control by Contempt

In the 2009 film *Precious*, sixteen-year-old Claireece Precious Jones lives in a home where conversation consists of issuing orders and abuse. As soon as she enters the home, she is told to cook, to clean, to attend to others' needs. At the same time, she is proclaimed to be "a dummy-don't-nobody-want-you-don't-nobody-need-you-girl." Still in junior high and pregnant with her second child, Precious is used by her parents as a servant, a whipping post, a scapegoat, and an object for occasional, brutal lust. Precious's own needs do not register in her parents' thoughts or actions. This film is a powerful and deeply disturbing portrayal of abuse—sexual, physical, emotional. In bold strokes it outlines how contempt and control interact; a parent may justify her control with contempt: your needs and wishes and views are worthless, and therefore I, the parent, am justified in controlling you.

Fourteen-year-old Elsa's experience is very different from that of Precious. There is no physical abuse, but she is overwhelmed by the minute-to-minute control and criticism from her mother, Lavinia. For this mother/daughter pair, conversation consists of orders issued by Lavinia and back talk from Elsa. In response, Lavinia repeats her original orders and adds new orders to the list, interjecting criticism in her commands. Lavinia begins by telling Elsa to clean her room; Elsa says she will clean it in a minute; Lavinia instructs her to clean it now and to make sure the clean clothes are in drawers or on hangers and that the floor is swept. She tells Elsa that she is always slow to do as she is told and that she is lazy. While Elsa stares at her computer screen, pretending to be impervious to her mother's criticism, Lavinia tells her to close down the computer, to stop using her phone, and to substitute her unhealthy breakfast with a better diet. As Elsa begins to sort out her room, Lavinia follows her, watches her, and continues to instruct her: "Pick up the towels first. I told you to hang them on the rail, not the end of the bed. How many times have I told you that? And now you have to get your butt in gear and get it to school. Do you want to be late? Again? Are you going to make me write another note to the teacher? And on the way home go to the post office, the one on the way home, not the one near Sadie's house, and don't you dare forget to mail my package."

Each instruction by itself is reasonable enough, but collectively and cumulatively they frustrate and humiliate Elsa. Directives come thick and fast. They saturate the environment. "I can't think when she talks like that," Elsa tells me. "She takes away my mind. There's nothing left. Only her words going: bang, bang, bang."

Dilemma: Voice or Exit

Lavinia tells me, with sincerity, that she exerts control in the name of love. She worries that Elsa is "headstrong" and that her willfulness will "destroy her." Elsa is sometimes reported by her school as being truant. Lavinia suspects that her fourteen-year-old daughter is sexually active, and she is trying to guide and protect her. However, guidance and protection are expressed through commands, criticism, and the cynical rejection of Elsa's own views.

Elsa confronts a choice between voicing her resistance to her mother or exiting a genuine relationship. If she voices her resistance, she is being honest but the conflict increases. Her mother's response to conflict is to clamp down. So as Elsa tries to speak out, she is subject to further control. Her strategy is therefore to exit a genuine relationship. She complies with many of her mother's demands, but she has no regard for them when her mother is not looking in her direction. She remains in a shell relationship, where she "follows orders when Mom is watching and get away with what I can." She produces cover stories for truancy and late nights. "My mom doesn't have the slightest idea who I really am," she says. "And by hiding who I am, I can just about get by."

Lying is a common strategy to resist maternal control. It is a way of avoiding "trouble" and open conflict without total compliance. In these circumstances, lying becomes so routine that children lie about everything, even when a lie serves no purpose.

They may lie about where they are going, what they are doing, and what they are thinking. The underlying assumption is, "To have the freedom to do some of the things I like doing, or to be friends with people I like, or just to have some relief from constant orders, I have to hide who I am and what I want from my mother." But lying also signals a decision to exit the relationship rather than to work within it and adjust it to the child's own needs. Elsa maintains "the peace" by hiding who she really is rather than negotiating better relational terms with her mother. She maintains harmony by hiding; she preserves the "relationship" by exiting a real relationship of mutual engagement.

In her seminal book *My Mother, Myself*, Nancy Friday describes how her mother's refusal to acknowledge her daughter's individuality and sexuality made a genuine relationship impossible. Instead, her mother's attempt to control her by denying her feelings and desires led to a relationship characterized by mutual lying and distrust. Friday faced a dilemma in which her choice was between limiting her sexual self—along with the adventurousness and confidence associated with desire—and trusting and finding comfort in her mother. The compromise resulted in mutual deception: "I have always lied to my mother, and she to me." Friday reflects and mourns for the loss of a possible, open conversation in which mother and daughter could look at each other eye to eye. For Nancy Friday, as for Elsa, lying is a compromise strategy. It avoids arguments by presenting a false self. Moreover, Friday notes that lying is mutual; the mother who does not resonate with a child's honest voice and yet purports to love her child is in effect lying.

No child needs or could reasonably have a mother's endorsement of every desire. All children need a parent's input in regulating their impulses. They need to tolerate frustration, to learn patience, and to prioritize long-term goals over immediate satisfaction. But when a parent sees a child's will as bad and dangerous, when a child's inner states are treated as corrupt, then a child is left with confusion and self-doubt. Instead of showing curiosity and delight in a child's good self, the controlling parent instills guilt. Instead of acting as a sounding board for a child's developing self, the controlling parent dampens all resonance with the child. The controlling parent claims expert knowledge of who a child is and what a child wants and needs. As the expert, the parent refuses to listen and learn from the child. As the expert, the parent sees her role as director and controller of her child. This complex endeavor to break a child's will is described by the psychoanalyst Alice Miller as "poisonous pedagogy."

Who Owns My Story?

The neuroscientist Antonio Damasio makes an illuminating distinction between a core self and an autobiographical self. The core self is grounded in our own individual responses and desires, feelings that are deeply personal and specific to us. Our brains are wired to observe the world around us. Moment by moment, we register what we see and give meaning to our experiences, not always consciously but emotionally and physically. Damasio likens this to a film running continually inside us, and our awareness of watching the film provides a sense of time and continuity: this is what we feel, what we remember, who we are, and how we have changed.

The autobiographical self is the more public story we hear or tell about our self. The autobiographical self is vulnerable to distortion and denial. Sometimes we, and the people around us, build up false stories about who we are. If we become wedded to a false story of our self, there is a disconnect between what we think we want, who we think we should be, and what we really feel and what we really know deep down. Normally we revise this autobiographical self as we make decisions about our way forward. Significant people (particularly a mother) can impede this readjustment.

Children delight in hearing stories about when they were a baby, and they often depend on their parents for understanding stories about themselves and the family. As a parent fills in some of the missing chapters of a child's autobiographical self, the child learns how stories are told, how they can be imbued with meaning and interest, and how different events and actions are linked. But a child also needs the freedom to write his or her own story—one that is shaped by the developing core self. In healthy conditions, the autobiographical self is shaped by the core self and can support the richness of the core self. When a parent runs interference on this delicate process of interaction, a son or daughter feels trapped in the parent's rigid version of the autobiographical self. The core self's consciousness grows slack and sullen, and the child begins to lose touch with his or her own unique register of experience.

A controlling parent tries to take charge of both the child's core self and the autobiographical self. The child's moment-to-moment experiences are disrupted by a parent's repeated intrusion. She commands the child what to see, feel, and want. She constantly intrudes on his own moment-to-moment experiences. As she takes ownership of him, the child loses touch with his own inner states. The consequent questions are: Why is my parent unwilling to revise her view of me? Do I have to adhere to her story to be acceptable? Does she really know the truth about me better than I do? Am I capable of knowing what I want?

Normally a child resists a parent's attempt to become the expert on what he or she wants. "I haven't wanted that since I was seven!" a thirteen-year-old barks, offended by a mother's outdated views. These corrections are often rough and clumsy, particularly during adolescence. But within this rough and tumble comes vitality. A growing child is alive to new possibilities. "Take a new look at me," the son or daughter pleads, hoping that eventually a parent will see him or her in a new light. No parent always enjoys these demands, but a controlling parent sees them as evil.

The difference between healthy and necessary parental control and poisonous control lies in its character, focus, and purpose. Healthy control shapes general values and sets down specific rules; but it is informed by listening in the broadest sense, and it respects a growing child's ability to fill in the details of life's general requirements. A difficult mother's control is based on an idée fixe that implies on a daily basis: "I know who you are, and you don't" or "I need you to be this, and that is more important than what you want."

Enmeshment as Control

Control is not always coercive. Sometimes it creeps in and takes hold with no outward sign of cruelty. A parent simply takes ownership of a child's thoughts and feelings, and the child is given a choice between shaping himself in the parent's image and following the parent's constant stream of instructions, on the one hand, or being the target of the parent's anxiety and disapproval, on the other. Instead of listening for her child's cues, the parent sees her child's heart and mind as vessels to be filled with the parent's thoughts and feelings. Instead of showing sensitivity to a child's developing inner states, the parent sees herself as custodian and controller of her child's mind. The message is, "I need you to want/think/feel in this way" and "You are not allowed to change."

To please this parent, a child must develop what psychoanalyst Donald Winnicott calls a "false self." This is an autobiographical self written by the parent, shaped by the parent's wishes, and disconnected from the child's core self. Sometimes a controlling mother is unaware that there is any distinction between what she wants and what her child wants. Sometimes the mother's own insecurities make it difficult to trust her child's instincts. Self-doubt leads her to suppose that her child cannot function without her constant micromanagement. In whatever form, the blurring of boundaries between her own needs and goals and those of her child results in enmeshment. A mother ignores or marginalizes a son's or daughter's experiences because she does not realize that she is not the final authority on the child. Care and focus become coercive as she monitors her child's feelings and makes judgments on every thought or emotion because she sees the child's inner world as a satellite of her own.

Enmeshment generates extreme confusion. Children take a basic delight in their individuality. They probe and ponder ways they are similar to and different from the people they feel close to. When they ask for their own space, what they are seeking is uninterrupted reflection on personal boundaries and connections. When a mother fails to see that her child is a different person, the child comes to doubt their own subjective experience. Can what I feel be real when my mother "knows" my feelings and says they are different from what I think they are? Am I unknown to her because my core self is unacceptable?

Below are three snapshots—two of young adults and one of a young teen—of people who struggle to know their own minds, impeded because a mother think she knows it for them.

Craig is a recently discharged marine trying to find some way to readjust to civilian life. At the age of twenty-three, he craves supportive understanding from his mother, who has always held him to a "gold standard" and who "refuses to hear about [his] inner turmoil." Though he is trained to act with disregard for his own physical safety, this relational dilemma fills him with a fear he says he "can't stand up to." His mother's "glassy eyes and closed ears" leave him "sick and empty and in free fall."

Gary, age nineteen, is trying to look past his failure in his freshman exams, but his mother insists that "he always wanted to be a mathematician," so changing course is out of the question. His mother attributes his failure to many things: his girlfriend, his recent bout of flu, his failure to follow the study regime she set out for him. What she does not consider, Gary says, is "all the things I try to tell her about what I really want to do. She asks, 'Why do you talk like that?' Then a minute later I'm getting one order shot at me after another. I can't think. I can't feel. All I see is her iron will."

As a family undergoes abrupt change, a difficult relationship may emerge from what was once a comfortable equilibrium. Joel's father had been a buffer between his fourteen-year-old son and his formidable mother. Following Joel's father's death, he and his mother, Paula, are struggling in very different ways with grief. Paula's determination to move on and put part of her life behind her leaves no room for the different rhythm of Joel's responses. She tells Joel that his depression is illness, and she hands him over to a therapist for treatment. Paula cannot let Joel grieve in his own way. "I don't know what I feel," Joel says. "I don't know if I feel anything. Mom comes between me and my feelings."

In a healthy relationship, a mother's response can help a son or daughter mentalize—understand, reflect on, and contextualize—his or her own thoughts and emotions. A controlling mother, on the other hand, harnesses a child's thoughts and feelings to her own.

Parenting in a Controlling Culture

A parent may try to break her child's will as she prepares the child for a controlling culture.

"What must a child be to have a viable life in society?" is a question every parent considers. Usually this question is approached broadly, with a range of possible outcomes. What is possible in a particular place at a particular time is considered alongside a child's own changing and expanding impulses, inclinations, and talents. Usually the parent's question opens a long and flexible conversation that is constantly adjusted to her growing child. When a parent focuses only on her own rigid goals and ideals, her child faces a dilemma. On one hand lies a parent's heartfelt belief that the child's best interests are being considered; on the other hand is total disregard for the child's own desires. "What is best for my child?" then becomes an inflexible front on which images of care and love are painted while a child's core self is ignored.

In a competitive society, where people with skills, talents, experience, education, and training often vie for success, some parents control a child through a relentless schedule of academic tutoring, art classes, sports, and organized play. A parent defends her control by appealing to her child's best interests, but a child may experience something very different. The parent's interests become fixed; the battles between them become a vicious battle of will; and the coercive input may exhaust and deplete the child's own imagination and self-awareness.

Gender norms have throughout history been a focus for a parent's control. The parent herself may be facing a dilemma between exerting cruel constraint or failing to induct her child into social norms. In her short story "A Visit from the Footbinder," Emily Prager describes the disfigurement that a mother and aunt inflict on a six-year-old girl, subjecting her active, healthy feet to the foot binder. The arches of her feet are broken and her toes are bound beneath the soles of her feet, inflicting lifelong pain and disability. Her mother oversees this process, certain that such control is in the girl's best interests. As an "expert" on the cultural assumption that a woman with natural feet is unfit for marriage, the mother is impervious to the girl's protest.

Social norms induce a parent's cruel control through the genital mutilation sometimes known as female circumcision. Alice Walker and Pratibha Parmar in *Warrior Marks* explore the social and religious customs often upheld by mothers. In the name of love, they are accomplices in the infliction of cruel control over their daughters. A child's shattering sense of betrayal is discounted; her protests are illegitimate; her resistance is seen as "willful" or "bad." In these circumstances, a mother is "difficult" alongside many other forces in her child's life. The mother herself is controlled by others; but from a child's perspective, her mother is the person she looks to for protection. When a mother controls rather than protects, the child feels both silenced and furious.

Foot binding and female circumcision are obvious cases of coercive control; but there are less obvious practices that remain embedded in contemporary cultures. Ordinary loving mothers sometimes close down vital communication as they induct a daughter into a society that places cruel restrictions on their sexual and intellectual lives. To this end, a mother may exert control and punish self-assertion, outspokenness, individuality, and honesty.

Masculine norms may also require a parent's exercise of poisonous pedagogy. As a mother prepares her son to be manly, she may discourage affectionate connection; she may express disappointment or derision when he shows fear or sadness. From holding his own on the playground to fulfilling his role in the military, a mother may worry that her son's tenderness and vulnerability undermine his social standing. Thinking that her son cannot thrive if he does not follow the male code of independence, fearlessness, and aggression, she may sever the bond between them in order to "make him into a man." For both daughters and sons, a parent's imposition of social norms may inflict a controlling mother's dilemma: "Either comply with this template or be unacceptable, disappointing, and hateful to me."

Auditing Our Relationship and Its Effects

Mothers are individual people with their own histories, values, idiosyncrasies, and personalities. They have their own strong views about what a child should do, how a child should behave, and what suits a child's talents, interests, and needs. A special maternal knowledge, based on a history of intimate responsiveness, is often deep and true, but it requires flexibility and updating to remain true. As a child grows and develops, a parent who claims to know the child has to keep up by listening, in the broadest sense. When a son or daughter feels unknown and unseen, when his or her voice is not heard, when a parent tries to control a child's story, that child is vulnerable to self-doubt and confusion; his or her core self can be obscured even from their own view.

IF YOU ARE dealing with a dilemma related to a parent's control, you may struggle with a form of self-doubt in which your desires seem suspect and the prospect of making independent decisions fills you with anxiety.

- Do you freeze or fill with dread when you approach a decision?
- Do you hear a voice giving dire warnings even on minor matters, such as which train to catch, which selection to make in a restaurant?
- Do you ask yourself how you feel about something, and then go blank?

- Do you suppose that other people are judging you, on both small and large matters?
- Are you frequently nervous about what other people are thinking of you?
- Do you frequently find that lying about yourself is easier than telling the truth?
- Do you generally feel that there are many aspects of yourself that you have not begun to consider, let alone develop?
- Do you panic or go blank when you are asked to think outside the box?

If you are a teenager, then answering yes to these questions may be age related. If you have recently made some unfortunate life decisions, then answering yes to three or more of these questions might be a short-lived response to a recently disturbing event. But if these marks of self-doubt seem embedded in your personality, it would be helpful to consider whether you think you are still dealing with a controlling mother's dilemma.

Even as an adult, living in your own home, no longer subject to your mother's daily controls over things both small and large, you may have internalized the dilemma. It is possible, however, at any time of life to gain new understanding in ways that can help manage your own responses. You may also find other listeners and develop self-reflection and expression through close connections to a father, sibling, friend, or lover. When you can identify how the relationship with your mother was difficult and how it has affected you, you can hone your resistance to its negative effects.

There is no simple route to resilience. It may be helpful to go back to basics as you identify what you want and what you think.

The initial step is to observe and consider and listen to yourself, noticing what appeals to you, what attracts you, and what feels easy and comfortable. Holding "your mind in mind"—attending to your minute-by-minute observations and responses—will fill in those blanks in your mind.

There are also many positive traits you may have learned by negotiating a mother's control.

- Do you reflect on your thoughts and reveal them only when you are sure about them and sure you can defend them?
- Are you able to evaluate other people's fixed points and then stand back to consider ways of either leaving their judgments out of your decisions or finding a way around them?
- Are you able to "edit" a story—details you give to someone—without losing the full picture yourself?
- What is your response to a person who might be described as controlling? (a) Do you avoid that person as a close friend, or (b) Are you particularly attracted to controlling people?

If these traits apply to you, then it is likely you have not only weathered the effects of a difficult relational dilemma but also put some hard lessons to good use.

Chapter Five

THE NARCISSISTIC MOTHER

A BABY LEARNS the joy of connection when his mother meets his gaze and shows her curiosity and delight. Other people throughout our lives contribute to our sense of who we are, but that first powerful connection has a special impact. "See me," a child calls out as he pushes a swing all by himself. "Look!" he calls as he completes a puzzle. Whether he is drawing, building a tower of blocks, running, or cutting his own food, a child searches out a parent's attention and pleasure in his developing self.

Later in childhood we demand a more complex response. We become critical and exacting: "You're not paying attention!" and "It's private; leave me alone!" In the teen years, we increase the challenge to a parent's way of seeing. The common complaints about a mother—"She just doesn't see," "She won't listen," "She can't understand"—that litter teenage talk arise from a combination of high expectations and frustration. The teen hopes to update his parent's view of how he has changed from the child the parent thinks she knows. Sometimes the contradictory teen is certain that his parent is incapable of understanding his complex world; he simultaneously resents her failure to see into his heart and craves more privacy. Whatever our age, we remain particularly sensitive to a mother's view, and her gaze remains a reference point in our lives.

When the mirroring process is distorted by a mother's own needs, fears, or limitations, the child loses out on an important source for self-reflection. In this chapter I look at mothers who demand that their children mirror them at twice their natural size and reflect a reassuring, flattering, aggrandizing image.

The voices of the men and women who describe their experience with the dilemma of a difficult mother come from the 176 people who have participated in my research on teenagers and parents, adults and their parents over the course of the past fifteen years. Of these 176 people, 35, just over 20 percent, describe a history of dealing with a difficult mother. Out of these 35 people, 11, just under one-third, describe a mother in ways suggesting behavior that can be called "narcissistic."

Big Ego or Fragile Self?

Narcissus in Greek legend was a young man so absorbed by his own beauty that he was unable to love and admire anyone but himself. As he reached into a pool of water to embrace his own image, he was drowned.

In everyday usage, a "narcissist" is a person who is totally self-involved. Narcissists' conversation is all about themselves.

They seriously overestimate their achievements. They exaggerate their importance to other people. While their sense of superiority may seem perfectly intact, it requires constant bolstering. They demand admiration yet are always on the lookout for any failure to give them their due. They resent anyone who seeks attention or status or praise for themselves. Any other person's self-importance is an affront to theirs.

Everyone has some narcissistic needs and some narcissistic traits. Sometimes these are called *amour propre* or self-love. A healthy face of narcissism is simply self-worth. When we want people to notice that we've done something well, when we're pleased by compliments on a meal we've prepared or on how we look, we are in a broad sense seeking to satisfy our narcissistic needs. When we take pride in a job we have done, we savor a healthy narcissism.

Our need for others to bolster our self-worth will be more prominent at some phases of our life than at others. When we feel particularly low, we may need more attention. When a mother has little support elsewhere, she may demand more attention and appreciation from her children. *Narcissism* in the broadest sense is the need to be seen and appreciated, and this is part of being human.

The narcissist whose craving for recognition overreaches healthy levels is commonly thought to have a big ego, but in clinical psychology "narcissist" describes a person with a very fragile sense of self. The majority of people who have a clinical diagnosis of "narcissistic personality disorder" (NPD) are men, but the special difficulty a narcissistic mother poses arises from a child's need for a mother's focus and empathy.

Typically, a narcissist swings from grandiosity to abject insecurity. Feeling injured, humiliated, hollow, and empty, she reacts defensively. She is quick to attack whomever she supposes might be depriving her of the adoration she craves. She carefully monitors others' behavior for possible signs of criticism or disrespect. Any failure to idolize her is an affront to her. She is quick to hear a casual remark as a lack of appreciation or respect, and many apparently casual conversations result in a long-term grudge. She sees a remark that most people would find neutral as casting aspersions on her or insulting her. When another person expresses their view, she may feel outraged that she is not allowed the sole and final word on a subject. She may actually go out of her way to engage in furious arguments as a means of trumpeting her outrage and punishing others for failing to acknowledge her superiority. In a fever of anger, she thrills with contempt for others. The underlying message is, "You may think you are something, but I have nothing but contempt for you, so I am better than you."

It is hard to engage with a narcissist. However disproportionate her anger may seem to others, it is fully justified in her eyes. If you try to reason with her, you are likely to anger her further. If you see things differently, then you offend her. She operates on the assumption that anyone who is not fixed in admiration is attacking her.

In a narcissistic mind-set, the mother is largely unable to show her child the mutuality and responsiveness that is central to a healthy relationship. Instead of reflecting the child's inner states, she demands that her child reflect an aggrandized image of her. Every request for attention becomes a competition. For example, when a child complains of being tired or disappointed, he may be told, "Don't talk to me about feeling tired. I'm so tired that it hurts. I've been hard at work all day. You don't know what being really tired is," and "I don't want to hear about your disappointment. You should think about what I've been through."

But she also sees her child as part of her; therefore her child must be outstanding to be worthy of her. The child is under pressure both to be subservient to the mother's superiority and to shine for her on her terms. Volatility, confusion, and endless bewildering demands are all familiar to those who live in this difficult relational environment. Children who confront this dilemma generally do so through one of two broad strategies: appeasement or rebellion.

Placating a Narcissist

Children want to please their parents. In spite of a two-year-old's petulance, a seven-year-old's naughtiness, and a fifteen-year-old's hubris, sons and daughters are more content when they believe that a parent is pleased with them. If a mother demands that a child adore her, then initially the child complies. But a narcissist's needs can never be satisfied; the craving for attention and adoration comes from an unstable self, and any satisfaction is short-lived. The dilemma—fulfill my needs or I'll treat you with disdain—demands constant effort. Any success in compliance is short-lived, and the child lives under a constant cloud of disdain regardless of his or her efforts.

A narcissist seems assured of her worth, but in reality she feels on the edge of collapse. This makes her relationships fragile. Children of a narcissistic parent often feel that the entire relationship can break apart at any minute. They may constantly be on guard lest they inadvertently offend her. A child's routine challenges and criticisms—particularly in the teen years—present inordinate threats to a narcissistic mother, who is likely to respond with pain and fury: her child does not show her proper love and respect; her child is not worthy of her love. Since a child of a narcissist is likely to witness a mother's frequent and final rejections of friends, neighbors, and siblings for "insulting" her in some way, the child knows that the potential for rejection is real.

Many children try to appease a parent's unregulated narcissism. They flatter her. They show deference. They put her feelings first. But their best efforts offer at most transient satisfaction, and the relationship as a whole remains unstable. At the age of thirty-two, Sandra's memory of her mother's vacillation from inflated to deflated ego is vivid and visual:

> When I said just the right thing she would pull herself up and love seemed to pour out of her mouth and eyes. When I was a real young kid this thrilled me, but I soon learned that her gush of love would turn into a torrent of abuse. Something I did or said would inevitably offend her, and then her whole body would shake. I can see her now: breath drawn in, chin raised, backbone taut. Her eyes became weapons, sharp and cruel, because I deserved the arrows that she wanted to shoot in my heart. I knew the words before they were uttered: "How dare you?" and "Just who do you think you are?" and of course, "If you're going to treat me like that, you're gonna have to leave this house."

Though Sandra in many respects is competent and self-assured, part of her remains vulnerable to her mother's contempt. Many children of a narcissistic mother develop a highly critical inner voice; this is an internalized version of their mother's voice, burned into their brain as a neuro-linguistic program. This switches on whenever there is a hint that something has gone wrong—whether it is a slight awkwardness in a conversation or a small glitch in an everyday skill. Sandra describes a self-battering voice: "I call myself 'stupid' and 'useless.' I tell myself that I don't deserve anything, and that I'll die a failure."

When this neuro-linguistic program runs riot, a son or daughter of a narcissistic mother experiences what is called "the collapse." The internal voice wages a global attack, however minor and specific its trigger. This internal programming derives from the self-loathing that a narcissistic mother pours into a child. Since a narcissistic parent is likely to feel empty herself, she may try to make others feel even more inadequate. She then looks at the person she has reduced and is able to tell herself, "At least I am better than you."

Enabling a Narcissist

An enabler helps a narcissist uphold her delusions. He or she endorses the narcissist's view that anyone who criticizes her or challenges her or admires someone else more than her is committing an offense. An enabler also endorses the narcissist's thrill of emotion as she savors a triumph or condemns an insult.

Sometimes as a child participates in his mother's inner world, he becomes trapped within her dramas. Stepping out of that role is difficult, because the child does not know any other interactive script. Paul, now age thirty-seven, was for many years his mother, Pat's, chief admirer. He saw her just as she needed to be seen: "I was convinced everyone who met her loved her instantly. I thought she was wonderful." When Paul turned sixteen and started dating, however, the fragile side of his mother's narcissism came into play. She accused him of harboring negative thoughts about her: "You think I'm just an old, useless woman." She attacked him for no longer loving her or respecting her. He found that the only way to manage her vulnerability and her coldness was to adopt once again the child's adoration and dependence.

Now Paul is passively watching his marriage of two years fall apart. "I can't get my wife to see that when Mom needs me, I have to see her. When my mom needs something, I have to give what I can. There's too much at stake there to say no." But his wife sees a different problem: "It's not the time he gives Pat, but the fact that he pretends I'm not there. He has eyes only for her. He snaps at me when I talk to him in her presence. He always dances to her tune."

A narcissist is unlikely to see why someone she loves might have need for anyone besides herself. But because she is not conscious of this mind-set, she can deny vociferously and sincerely that she is trying to limit her child; at the same time, all her words and actions continue to express her wish to have him all to herself.

The Child as a Proxy for a Parent's Narcissism

Children, with their remarkable capacity to learn and observe, with their physical beauty and natural charm, easily gratify a parent's healthy narcissism. "What a beautiful child I have!" many parents think. It is easy to be so absorbed in our own delightful child that we pity other parents because they have less wonderful children.

"What an awful child I have!" is another common thought, as a child deals a blow to our narcissism by throwing a tantrum in the supermarket checkout, by being the least well behaved at a family gathering, by being the slowest reader in his class.

Most parents moderate their narcissistic needs as they engage in the scramble and sparring involved in raising a child, though regulating *amour propre* is easier at some phases of a child's life than at others. A baby, full of love and longing for a parent, fixing his adoring gaze on a parent, assures a parent of her significance and worth. A child's acceptance of a parent's power and knowledge, and his eagerness to imitate and learn from a parent, is gratifying. The teen years may present a challenge to any parent. A teen's arch criticism is wounding, but most parents quickly heal and forgive. In a narcissistic mother's mindset, however, the rough and tumble of life with a child who is honing his own independence is intolerable. The son or daughter is seen as "bad" or "wicked" because he or she does not see how the mother "should" be treated. A son or daughter who wants to go their own way may also offend a narcissistic parent by failing to shine in the way the parent wants the child to shine.

A narcissistic mother demands deference and subservience; but at the same time, her child also may be expected to act like a narcissist. The child may find that the best way to appease a narcissistic mother is to take center stage and shine on a mother's behalf. The message is: "To appease my narcissism, you have to be admired by others because you are an extension of me."

Delight and Despair

Mona Simpson draws a compelling portrait of a narcissistic mother in her first novel, *Anywhere But Here*. Adele is a free spirit with a high opinion of herself and little regard for others. She is also a narcissist who demands two things from her daughter, Ann. First, she demands that Ann be an audience for her. Second, she demands that Ann herself become a star, because a star child is what Adele "deserves." Adele takes Ann away from the world she knows—from school, from her friends, and from the father and grandmother she loves—in order to pursue her own dream. The whirlwind relationship is both exhilarating and terrifying.

One of the most confusing aspects of a difficult mother is that the relationship is seldom all bad. The high expectations of a narcissistic parent can inspire her child to high achievements. There can also be aspects of a mother's personality that delight a child, and when these are in play the fear and pain vanish. A narcissist can exhilarate others with her thrilling self-delight and sense of adventure. Phil, age twenty-eight, describes his mother, Gail, as extravagant, impulsive, sophisticated, and stylish. "There were times when she made anything seem possible."

Yet that bubble is easily burst, and then the narcissist demands that anyone who wants to remain close to her has to meet her volatile needs. Should Phil decline any request, his mother threatens him with rejection. When a narcissistic mother threatens rejection, she tends to be true to her word. A narcissist is very like to hold a grudge, and forgiveness is granted only after the "culprit" begs repeatedly for forgiveness and takes all the blame on himself.

Different Children, Different Roles, Different Effects

A difficult mother is "difficult" in the context of a particular relationship and the responses of a particular child. Sometimes a mother projects her better feelings onto one child and her self-doubt onto another. In psychology, the term *projection* is based on the simple analogy of a device that projects an image contained in the device onto a wall or screen. It describes the common process of projecting something that belongs inside us onto someone else. The narcissist's defensive position—"I am wonderful, the best, the most important"—may be projected onto one child who is then seen as outstanding and magnificent; the narcissist's underlying position—"I am fragile, and easily shown to be worthless"—may be projected onto another child who is then denigrated. Often the recipient of the negative projection is a daughter; because she is the same gender as the mother, she receives the projection of a mother's underlying feelings. A son is more likely to receive the narcissist's grandiose projections; his clear difference from the mother makes it more likely that he will be a recipient of her fantasy images.

Even children of the same gender may be affected in different ways. Two sisters, Bev and Harriet, have very different experiences of the mother they share. Bev, thirty-six, reflects:

> My mother believes she's very different from other people. She is different and she is special and way, way better. As a kid, I had to be special and better because I was her child. If anyone else brags about their daughter, she's offended. She doesn't think other people have a right to be pleased with their children. They must be putting her down if they're pleased with something that belongs to them and not her. It's a real blow to her that there was never any chance of me being the brightest kid on the block.

Resisting this judgment, but knowing that her mother's judgment would never change, Bev took a careful look around her and deliberately resisted this mind-set. She decided that she could be satisfied with who she was and what she could do.

Harriet's response is very different:

When I got a medal for coming in second in a race, all she said was, "Oh." And there was a steely pause. Finally, she asked, with a real edge, "Who came in first?" All I can do is hope I'm first each time. Of course, usually I'm not. And then I feel worthless. I still shudder when I hear about a friend's or cousin's success. I know my mother will turn to me and demand, "Why did you let her do better than you?"

Every clinician I know has patients who view themselves as a failure because they have failed to satisfy the unsatisfiable demands of a parent. What takes a long time for a person in this position to realize is that no success is big enough or long-lasting enough to satisfy a narcissistic mother. Objective merit has little to do with meeting the demands of a narcissistic parent. Harriet would benefit from realizing that her mother's disappointment will be activated no matter what. Harriet thinks she can avoid this by staying in the spotlight.

Yet being in the spotlight is also dangerous because a child's success may be construed by a narcissistic mother as competition. In self-defense, a son or daughter may insist that any achievement is a fluke, that any award is undeserved or is really a tribute to their mother. They suppress their own healthy narcissism to please a mother who feels that she alone is allowed to shine, and become prone to what is called "the impostor syndrome." They believe that any success is a mistake and that at any moment they will be "found out" and identified as a fake or a fraud. The mind-set is, "I am succeeding because I can fake excellence, but inside I am not really worthy or not really able." Such self-effacement is common in people who are pressured to excel and also primed to assure others—such as that all-important narcissistic mother—that they are subservient and inferior.

Rebellion and Resolution

Appeasing a mother's narcissism—whether by placating her, enabling her, or becoming a proxy for her needs—carries various costs and involves various skills, but many who use this strategy are high functioning: they interact positively with others, contribute to society, and develop their talents. A second pattern of adaptation—rebellion—is self-destructive.

Jacqui's mother, Helena, is a successful professor of French literature. Her colleagues find her stimulating and provocative. Her students adore her and describe her as generous with her time and a wonderful mentor. Her daughter, now age sixteen, experiences her mother's success very differently. Like many people who face a difficult dilemma in this powerful relationship, Jacqui has acquired subtle insights into her responses to her mother's character. She is highly articulate about the quality of her own anger: "Her hauteur is like a vice. I succeed on her terms or I'm garbage. From the age of twelve, I could feel her disappointment stab me, and I stabbed right back." Jacqui distinguishes between her own perspective and that of others: "If she were my teacher, I'd think she was wonderful. I'd find her perverse originality exciting. Maybe she'd inspire me. But as a mother, she crushes me." Her insight, rather than moderating her anger, increases her frustration. "She'll never change. She'll never step back and see how things are for me. I'll always be the stupid girl who fails to live up to her genius."

Jagged scars cover Jacqui's arms. She has been hospitalized as a threat to herself, but this threat extends beyond the episodes of overdoses and wrist slashing. She seeks out people who humiliate her. She tries to swim to the bottom, rebelling against her mother's focus on the top.

Rebellion is different from resistance. A daughter or son who resists is seeking a positive way forward. A daughter or son who rebels is not working free from a parent, but seeking an awful revenge. In rebelling, Jacqui deliberately messes up her own life to shame her mother.

Chaos at the Heart of Narcissism

Most of us have to deal with a narcissist at some point in our lives. Perhaps at work we have a colleague who demands special attention and constant flattery, and who cannot see anyone else's need for support. Perhaps we have a neighbor who rushes into our home with endless news about herself, delivered with a sense of urgency because she assumes we are hungry to hear about every detail of her life. Usually we feel left out in the cold by a narcissist's demanding self-image; but sometimes a narcissist buoys up our own mood. In spite of being high maintenance, a narcissist can exude energy and confidence. But for a son or daughter, who cannot close their mind's door against a parent, narcissism is deeply confusing. Children may have real admiration and love for a parent, but over and over again they will be told that their admiration and love fall short of what is due to her. They may enjoy a mother's self-delight when she is "up" but be burdened by her demands for attention and reassurance in her more anxious phases. Overwhelmed by the requirement to focus on her, they are bewildered as to how to establish their own sense of significance.

Postcards from the Edge, the 1990 film based on Carrie Fisher's semi-autobiographical novel about her life with her mother, the actress Debbie Reynolds, shows the confusing mix of delight and exasperation with a narcissistic mother. When Suzanne Vale (played by Meryl Streep) takes a drug overdose and nearly dies, her mother, Doris Mann (played by Shirley MacLaine) comes to visit her in the hospital. The first show of concern for her daughter is rapidly overtaken by concern about her appearance: "What's happened to your hair?" Doris demands.

Like most narcissists, Doris sees everything in terms of its effect on her. When Suzanne accuses her mother of failing to take in what has happened, Doris brushes her daughter's feelings aside and reports that she is the one who has suffered most. She lapses further into self-pity as she tries to read Suzanne's mind: "I suppose you're going to blame me for this," she whines. Then she launches into a new attack on her daughter for her failure to succeed.

Suzanne receives the divided message familiar to any child of a narcissist: "You must be a star to be worthy of me, but you must never be as good as me." Suzanne is both a high achiever and a self-defeater. She has talent, but she constantly messes up. She turns up to work drunk or drugged. She falls for men who are likely to demean her. But the story does not end in this stalemate. The feel-good movie concludes as Suzanne discovers she can love her mother without aggrandizing her. Once she gains sufficient perspective her mother shrinks to a normal human size and Suzanne can find her own voice. She can sing in her own style, without fearing that her mother will punish her success.

Is there any way that others who confront a narcissistic mother can avoid Suzanne's many setbacks and patterns of self-defeat? Is there a quicker route to self-acceptance? Below are some guidelines for speeding the process of recovery.

Auditing the Effects of a Narcissistic Parent

If you have to negotiate a relationship with a narcissistic parent, you are likely to feel that the relationship itself is inherently fragile. An emotional audit involves consideration of these questions:

- Are you accustomed to a rush of praise from a parent, followed by explosive and global criticism?
- Do you feel you have to take great care what you say to your mother?
- Does every problem, whether in the family or in the world, turn into her dramatic crisis?
- Does your mother's mood dominate everything?
- Do her feelings always take precedence?

If you have had to deal with this dilemma—"Either submit to my needs or be the target for my disappointment and derision"—then you are likely to have adapted to it by either some form of appeasement or rebellion. Appeasers placate a narcissistic mother's fury and self-doubt, or they shore up her belief in her superiority, or they place their own hard-won successes before her as tributes. Becoming a proxy for a narcissistic mother's self-aggrandizement is a difficult double act. You have to shine, but you cannot outshine her. You have to take center stage, but you cannot upstage her.

IF YOU HAVE adapted by some version of appeasement, then you are likely to have a range of characteristics, some of which are useful and some of which probably make you miserable. Among the useful traits you may have acquired are:

- Diplomacy: you are very careful about making your point.
- Patience: you know how to sit tight when someone is fuming because you've learned that standing up for yourself or interrupting an indulgent release of contempt will make matters worse.
- Perfectionism (the upside): you set high standards and feel pressure to confirm one success by achieving another.
- Wisdom: while some people are attracted to characteristics they are used to, even characteristics that have caused them a great deal of pain, you may have special antennae for certain "impossible" people. You are wary of getting too close to someone who seems genial but shows contempt for others. You are wary of someone who seems genial but tells stories that always show him in the spotlight.

You may also have self-defeating patterns of thought and behavior:

- The impostor syndrome: you constantly explain away your achievements and think people who think well of you are making a mistake.
- Unrealistic standards for yourself but not others: you think that if someone else has achieved more than you have by some measure, then others' achievements totally wipes out the value of anything you have achieved.
- Deference: your impulse is to be deferential to people,

and you work hard to show them that you are willing to admire them. Perhaps you also feel that others will attack you if you display self-confidence.

- Perfectionism (the downside): you focus on your errors or flaws and give these far more weight than you give positive results of your efforts.
- Self-punishment: an inner voice is easily triggered that lashes out at you, issuing dire warnings that ever-increasing disasters will result from your behavior.
- Self-sabotage: when you are on the cusp of a significant achievement, you do something to sabotage your chances. Perhaps you are afraid to show that you can be as good as or better than your parent.

If you have adapted by rebellion, then you are likely to engage in an extreme version of self-sabotage. You seek revenge by putting a parent to shame, but at a huge cost to yourself. If you identify with any of the patterns listed below, then you need to engage in a paradigm shift. Your survival does not lie with these strategies:

- Do you frequently mess up opportunities, either by missing appointments or by poor planning?
- Do you tend to disappoint people who try to champion you?
- Do you feel comfortable being subservient to people who claim to be superior?
- Do you form relationships with people who humiliate you?
- Are you terrified when you have a success, however small?

Using the Audit to Move Forward

Can you see how these traits have arisen in response to a difficult relationship with your mother? When the traits you dislike are put into context, they become far more manageable because you see they serve no purpose.

Imagine saying something like this to yourself:

I am trying to protect myself from the punishment my mother would inflict if she thought I was proud of my own achievements. I understand that she expected a lot of me because she wanted her child to shine, but at the same time she resented anyone else taking pleasure in their own achievements. I see that this is incoherent and problematic, and I have to free myself from this paradox.

Another problem you may face is that other people's successes fill you with anxiety. Perhaps you think:

My mother wanted to be seen as superior, and she was offended by others' bids for attention. When other people are singled out for an award or recognition, I worry that my mother will be upset with me for not stealing the limelight. I see that the superior status she valued was really very fragile. I've internalized anxiety that I might implode if someone else earns the limelight. But I can relearn this pattern because I realize that other people's successes and talents do not take anything away from me.

Here are things to consider:

Perhaps you wish you could take more enjoyment in others' talents and achievements.

Anyone can be momentarily rattled by the sudden success of a friend or neighbor, but someone who has adapted to a narcissistic mother by imitation is likely to be consumed by a flood of anxiety. Does this describe your response? Do you feel that you are inwardly collapsing when someone you know enjoys a success? Do you regret the fact that it is difficult to feel pleased about a friend's success?

Writing a list of things that give you pleasure and in which you take pride can help focus on the simple fact that another person's success or self-delight does not take away what you have.

Perhaps you notice that other people glaze over when you talk about yourself and your successes, and that instead of thinking they are bad you actually have sympathy for their viewpoint.

You may have developed the habit of telling stories in which you shine because that kind of conversation has been normal in the past. You could test this by writing out a typical conversation. There is nothing wrong with seeking reassurance and recognition from people from time to time, but this is not the only purpose of conversation. Try paying attention to what you enjoy when others speak. New conversational styles are easy to learn, as soon as you become aware of them.

Perhaps you struggle with the sense that everything you value and everything you take pride in disappears when you make even the smallest social error.

This fragility is a legacy of growing up in a relationship of unregulated narcissism, particularly if your mother projected her self-doubt onto you and found anything less than perfection intolerable. It can help to write down what any internal self-punishing voice says. Setting it out in the open may expose the punishing criticism for what it is: extreme and absurd. Try writing a very different script, with a broader view.

Chapter Six

THE ENVIOUS MOTHER

A PARENT'S RESPONSE provides a child with a wealth of life-shaping information. Her face provides a reflection, but one that reveals more than a mirror. Normally, when we venture into the world and hone our skills, we are backed up by a parent's faith in us. Her delight boosts our confidence and allows us to believe in ourselves. But in some cases, a child's joy or ability or opportunity becomes a source of resentment and anxiety. Instead of bolstering a child's confidence and inspiring a child with a sense of his own potential, a difficult mother begrudges her child independence and pride. Instead of sharing a child's pleasure, the parent demands: "Why can she feel joy when I don't?" or "Why does he have a chance to be successful when I have been disappointed?" or "What if his success means that he'll leave me?"

A difficult mother's envy betrays the most basic terms of the emotional contract with her child.

ENVY IS ONE of the most unpleasant feelings in the human register of emotions, both for the person who envies and for the person who is envied. A parent who envies a child is almost always unaware of her envy. She disguises it from herself with a range of other explanations for her displeasure: "You think too much of yourself," she accuses, and "It's my job to remind you what's what," or "Your hopes are too high; you're headed for disappointment."

Envy's Double Bind

Normally, parents long to see their children happy and with some measure of success. But in a particular, distorted mind-set a child's success and happiness arouse hostility. Glowing with good news, a son or daughter expects a parent's face to reflect admiration; instead, the parent's jaw freezes, the corners of her mouth pull down in a spasm of contempt. "Someday you'll realize you're not such hot stuff," a mother warns. Or perhaps the initial response is cheerful, but later you notice that ordinary things you do irritate her. "Stop making such a racket" and "Why do you have to go on and on about it?" Or perhaps you notice that she falls ill, gets a headache, or becomes morose just at the point where you hope your happiness will be shared.

Eventually, you learn that a parent's irritability, disdain, or sullen mood is linked to your pleasure or success, and you experience the strange phenomenon that has been called fear of success, where you understand that success results not in the reward of satisfaction but in ridicule and rejection. Since your parent is herself unaware of her envy, she may declare with conviction, "Of course I want you to succeed. Nothing would make me happier." You continue to seek success in the hope of pleasing her, but find that every prize you earn causes offense.

This double message, with its paralyzing split between what has a false tone and what rings true but is also deeply disturbing, creates what is called a double bind. Here a parent gives two different and opposing messages about how to behave, each wielding an emotional punch. The first message is: "I will be happy and love you if you prove yourself capable and confident"; but the second message, conveyed through coldness, withdrawal, or moroseness, is: "I will punish you if you enjoy good fortune."

Children have a quick subconscious grasp of envy's ugly force. They recognize it when they see it in a parent and are terrified by it. The pioneering psychoanalyst Melanie Klein described infantile love and rage as a product of primitive envy. In Klein's model, the infant's fragile ego is outraged whenever a mother seems to withhold anything the child wants. The infant sees the mother as the source of all his needs. His total dependence leads to extreme demands, and he wants total control over her. Klein believed that the infant's love for a mother initially contains violent, ambivalent feelings. In order to keep a mother close, the infant wants to "devour" her so that the mother is "incorporated"—literally held inside the infant. At the same time, Klein argued, the infant wants to destroy a parent, to punish her for not being totally in an infant's control. In Klein's view, primitive envy arises from a wish to possess what we love and to destroy what we love because we can never possess it fully.

As the infant's ego becomes less fragile, envy subsides. The baby learns that he can survive even when he cannot control his parent. He learns that he can trust his mother to attend to him, even if she does not do so immediately. Most important, the child develops a more integrated and complex concept of his mother as a person with many aspects to her, and not just someone who serves his needs. The need for total control of his mother becomes less pressing as the baby develops into a child who is able to take steps to meet his own needs. Ordinary discomforts, such as hunger and fatigue, no longer flood him with fear.

Though children outgrow their infantile envy, they retain unconscious memories of it and sense its destructive force. When a sibling or a friend is envious, they feel uneasy. When a parent is envious, they are cast into a mystifying landscape, where it becomes impossible to distinguish between damage and repair, desire and dread.

It is, however, only after years of puzzlement and pain that a son or daughter with an envious mother realizes, "My mother resents my happiness and competence!" Hence, it was not until Peg Streep, the author of *Mean Mother*, was in midlife, with a nearly grown daughter of her own, that she could look back and understand the effect she had had on her mother. As a round-faced, curly haired girl filled with energy and curiosity, her easy delight in herself and her world infuriated her mother. The very characteristics of a child that most mothers savor are bitter to an envious mother.

"I Don't Want You to Have What I Can't Have"

For most mothers, a child's good qualities give her even more pleasure than her own. But sometimes a series of personal disappointments that she cannot process, forgive, or overcome leaves her susceptible to envy. She feels threatened when she sees someone enjoying life, enjoying happiness, or demonstrating confidence. Exuberance and energy, particularly in someone close to her, fill her with rage. By contrast, she feels deprived and blames her child for her awful feelings.

The rare distortions in maternal mirroring—the narcissistic mother and the envious mother—can arise when a mother, having had her own ambitions thwarted, resents her daughter's success. In *The Peppered Moth*, Margaret Drabble depicts a mother who in her youth was a high achiever, full of promise, and confident in her own imagination and intellect. When she takes what she sees as the socially necessary step of getting married, her intellect and imagination atrophy. Marriage and motherhood press her life into the rigid mold of 1940s domesticity. Over the years, living in the shadow of her former persona, she watches her brilliant daughter blossom. She has two conflicting messages for this young girl, who represents both who she once was and who she will now never become. The first is, "You must succeed on your own terms if you are going to find happiness." The second message is, "I shall heap disapproval on you when you do succeed." The daughter then muses, "You may think, why bother to achieve? You do well, and you end up miserable."

Some sons and daughters who meet with this bewildering response believe they harbor a terrible power. Why does a mother fear things that give them pleasure? Why do their best efforts seem to harm her? What is it in them that prompts this bewildering response? Fay, now age thirty-six, recalls her childhood belief that "I was full of some black magic I couldn't control," particularly when, in the midst of her delight or absorption, her mother's accusations would rain down on her.

This, in some form, is the paradox faced by a daughter or son who experiences a mother's envy: When you do well, you pose a threat to the relationship you depend on. Yet, if you do not do well, you disappoint the person you depend on.

The Rebound Effect

This paradox can result in a *rebound effect*. In medicine, a rebound describes the body's efforts to rebalance itself after a drug has been taken. In this process, the body may pull in the opposite direction of a drug. For instance, taking a sedative to help you sleep may send signals to the body to stimulate your flagging system. So, instead of helping you sleep, the sedative may keep you alert. You may then think you need more of the very drug that is producing the opposite effect from the one you want.

A similar pattern occurs when a mother says, "This is what I want for you," but expresses resentment when you get it. A child tries to please her mother by being smart or looking good or coming in first in school, sports, or music, but she discovers that her achievements are met with suspicion, anger, or disdain. The child may then redouble her efforts to please, only to fail again and again. Often a child persists in believing that the problem is that she is not good or successful enough, when the problem is that she is actually too good and too successful. Since an envious mother does not admit even to herself what she feels, she justifies her resentment in ways that shame and confuse her child. The child's shame and confusion may reassure her envious mother, and this strange cycle is reinforced.

Fourteen-year-old Tess tries to comply with her mother's instruction to "show that you can do as well as your sister." Tess tries to please her mother but feels she cannot match up to her younger sister Amber who is, Tess assures me, "prettier than Barbie, and everyone loves her." Tess says that, in contrast, she is "awkward and ugly." She says her mother complains that, whenever she is happy, she "gets too loud." Whenever Tess does well in school and presents a glowing report to show that she has been awarded "better grades even than Amber," her mother accuses her of "being a show-off."

The themes Tess describes—contempt for her pride or pleasure, critical comparisons with her sister—suggest a pattern of envy. Tess struggles to fit the puzzling and contradictory messages together. What does her mother really want from her? What is the basis for her disapproval? How can she defend herself against her mother's disappointment in her school record without opening herself to criticism about boasting? How far do her pleasure and pride, and her natural way of expressing these, threaten her relationship with her mother? Is this perverse dynamic a feature of all close relationships, or just with her mother? How can she answer these questions when her mother's double-bind messages cast doubt on her own judgment?

A difficult relationship is made worse by the child's inability to make sense of what is going on. When envy infiltrates an intimate relationship, that relationship becomes incoherent. Children realize that the good things in their lives offend, even harm, the person who matters deeply to them and whom they long to please.

Difference Is Dangerous

Envy is sometimes linked to enmeshment—the inability to distinguish between oneself and one's child. In an enmeshed relationship, a parent fails to get to know her own child. Instead of picking up cues from a child about his or her own thoughts and feelings, a parent makes assumptions about who the child is. Difference is either denied ("That's not who you really are") or seen as "silly" or "wrong" or "bad." Feeling threatened, a parent seeks to destroy her child's manifold individuality.

Suppose a mother cannot distinguish her own needs and feelings from those of her child. If her life is filled with dissatisfaction, she supposes that her child's life must also be unsatisfying. If she fears challenge and change, then her child too must avoid these things. When her child persists in being happy, curious, adventurous, or optimistic, she feels that her child is taunting her for what she herself lacks, Moreover, because she believes her child should not be different from her, she experiences the child's push to think differently, act differently, and pursue very different goals as a breach of their bond. She may truly believe that the child is betraying her simply by pursuing his or her own distinctive fulfillment.

There are times when a mother's dormant envy may suddenly become active. During the many years I have worked with young men and women in adolescence and the transition to adulthood, I have noticed a pattern in which a mother is suddenly struck by the fear that her son's or daughter's developing skills and knowledge will leave her behind. "Will my child still value me as he or she finds their own way in the world?" Usually, the unease that accompanies necessary losses linked to human growth and change are assuaged by appreciation of a child's thrilling youth and new individuality. But sometimes a child's eagerness to seek out experiences quite different from a mother's is unacceptable. In the grip of this relational panic, a mother wants to punish her child for moving on.

When a son or daughter experiences this sudden reversal— a good-enough relationship morphing into a difficult one—they sense conflict but cannot address it directly because envy always tries to disguise itself. A child internalizes a vague foreboding that what he or she seeks will lose meaning, that what they value will corrupt what they have. The young adult's motivation, which their mother may have encouraged and supported for many years, goes into freefall.

Komnan is the first person in his family to go to a university, and he has the additional pressure of being at a prestigious university. He reflects back to the time, only a few years before, when

> Mom was my greatest fan, the person who never ceased to put me first. When Dad died, another mother might have told me to be the breadwinner, but instead she helped me stay in school. Now she seems to resent my success. Everything I say she thinks is some "insult." She accuses me of not respecting her. She says I don't love her. She wonders whether she can have a place in her heart for a son like me. She says she doesn't recognize me anymore. But all I've done is what she dreamed I'd do one day. I've been trying to honor her and my father's memory. Now I feel better when I mess up than when I do well. Two years ago my whole career streamed before me. Now everything seems poisoned, and nothing makes any sense.

Komnan faces a dilemma between taking pride in his growth but putting a crucial relationship at risk, on the one hand, and keeping a relationship safe while suppressing his and his family's long-term goals, on the other. This tension can set up a lifelong puzzle: "What personal losses will I incur if I enjoy professional success?"

ENVY IS A bizarre distortion of admiration; instead of seeing a child's success as a source of pride and taking delight in a son or daughter who flourishes, an envious mother feels that a child's happiness takes something away from her. She feels she cannot relate to what is good in her child or what her child takes pleasure in, and so she wants (unconsciously) to destroy this. She believes that she can have a comfortable and secure bond with her child only if her child's sense of self-worth is as low as hers.

Leaving Is Difficult

Surprisingly, leaving a difficult mother can be a greater challenge than leaving a mother who offers comfort, respect, and support. An envious mother may make you feel so bad that your pour energy into making it up to her. You may stay behind, limit yourself, and live within the aura of her dissatisfaction because you blame yourself for inflicting unpleasant feelings on her.

An envious mother has a full armory for instilling guilt. Her weapons include:

Accusation. "You think too much of yourself" or "You're being a show-off" can turn a child's normal pride in his or her achievements into perceived flaws.

Denigration. A child is reminded that "there are lots of people much better than you." A sibling, a friend, or a long-dead relative may be set up as a standard the child can never hope to meet.

Debt collection. This includes reminders of others' sacrifices on your behalf. "Don't think you got here by yourself" and "Lots of people gave up a great deal for you."

Coldness and discontent. When a parent is reserved or unhappy when a child thrives, no words are necessary to instill in a child anxiety about the bad effect of the things he or she once saw as good.

Harbingers of doom. "You're headed for a fall" and "You know what happens to someone who flies too close to the sun?" and "High hopes just lead to disappointment" reinforce the general message that happiness and optimism are dangerous.

Medical emergencies. When a range of more subtle messages that "good is bad" are ineffective, an envious mother can resort to a medical emergency. The underlying message is, "Your happiness or growth or success is killing me."

Every experienced therapist I know has a story to tell about a mother who makes a suicide attempt in response to a son's or daughter's decision to move away. One colleague described a man who had left home at the age of fifty-nine, and only after his "suicidal" mother died of natural causes. Whenever he determined to move out, she attempted suicide, and guilt bound him to her.

When we feel guilty for being different, when we feel guilty for being individual, we may become suspicious of our core self—the self that registers our day-to-day feelings and own individual responses. Whatever we experience as ours, unique, personal, is suspect: "Is my achievement going to damage me?" we wonder as we reach for our goal. "Do I have a right to this?" we ask ourselves as we consider a place in college, a job offer, a travel opportunity. A mother's envy transforms what seems good into something harmful. This sets up an alarm system wherein what you desire and what common sense declares desirable—pleasure, excitement, interest, ambition—take on the guise of danger and damage.

Maternal Envy: A Cultural History

In the fairy tale "Snow White," a (step) mother (the queen) stands in front of a mirror and asks the mirror, "Who is the fairest of them all?" For many years, the mirror reassures the queen that she is "the fairest in all the land." But one day, as the queen ages and Snow White blossoms, the mirror declares, "Thou, queen, art fair, and beauteous to see, but Snow White is lovelier far than thee." At this, the queen turns pale with rage and envy, and orders a servant to kill Snow White.

Some psychologists see the envious queen's response as typical of mothers' unconscious responses to their daughters. In her influential book, *The Psychology of Women*, the pioneering psychoanalyst Helene Deutsch argued that a mother typically envies her teenage daughter. Deutsch believed that a mother's show of protectiveness and tenderness is envy in disguise. For the youthful bloom of a teenage girl marks a mother's decline into middle age. Later generations of writers in the 1970s and 1980s also believed that maternal envy was common and put it down to the generational change: a daughter now has far more opportunities than her mother did. If a mother felt socially marginalized and personally frustrated, she might once have found an ally in her daughter. But a daughter who makes her way into an exciting new world not only leaves her mother behind but also may spurn her and look down at her.

My own research, however, shows that though some mothers do feel envy, those who do are few and far between. I have observed mothers and daughters in many contexts over two and a half decades, and I have concluded that mothers are far more likely to delight in a daughter's beauty, opportunity, and achievement than to feel envious. A mother may be ambivalent about a daughter's beauty for a range of reasons: she sees that her daughter attracts many men and fears that they will not see past her beauty to the true person inside. A mother may be ambivalent about a daughter's drive and intelligence because she sees that these might complicate a daughter's life, knowing how exhausting and frustrating it can be to balance different needs and abilities. But these feelings of concern are very different from envy.

In a culture in which women have been valued primarily for their youth and beauty, a woman approaching midlife may feel uncertain about her own social standing as she compares her appearance to that of her daughter. In a culture in which a generation of women did not have the opportunity to develop their expansive needs—the need to meet challenges and solve problems, to develop and test a range of skills, to interact positively with their broader social environment—a mother may marvel at how she missed out on so much. But there is a vast difference between pangs of regret—or private mourning for opportunities left behind or, more poignantly, for opportunities that have been closed to you—and envy.

When envy invades a mother/child relationship, the effects are very different from healthy tussles about good life choices. The great medieval poet Chaucer said envy was like a terrible contagion, spreading from one thing to everything. "Certainly, then," he wrote in "The Parson's Tale," "envy is the worst sin there is. For truly, all other sins are sometime against only one special virtue; but truly, envy is against all virtues and against all goodnesses." In envying a child's beauty, opportunity, talent, or individuality, a parent may come to envy and resent everything the child has, everything she is. Envy breeds where there is systematic disappointment or deprivation, but it spreads to include every good thing about the person envied. A child who experiences a mother's envy has trouble finding any place in the relationship that is comfortable or safe.

Auditing the Effect of a Parent's Envy

A personal audit can assess strategies you might have learned to manage the envious mother's difficult dilemma. Some of these strategies may lead to skills:

- You may know how to charm people so that others feel good about your good qualities. In other words, you stave off envy with charisma. You may also show empathy to others and reassure them of their own importance.
- You may have the dual skill of recognizing envy and ignoring it. In short, you see what lies beneath a person's criticism or derision, and you refuse to be fazed by envy. You have learned that someone's resentment of your success has no impact on the outcome of your efforts.
- Perhaps you have learned how to champion others' abilities. Do you succeed by facilitating others' successes? Are you an agent or a teacher or a coach? You may have chosen these roles for a number of reasons, but one may be that you have been creative in exercising your talents and skills while avoiding the limelight.
- You may be a compulsive achiever as you seek but never find the one success that will please your envious mother.

It is also helpful to consider how your coping strategies might have held you back. An envious mother may have left you suspicious of your own pleasure, desires, and goals. The most common aftereffect of a parent's envy is a lingering fear of success. In some cases, fear of success leads to self-defeat. After all, a failure does not arouse envy.

- Do you find time and again that you are on track to succeed at something and then suddenly things fall apart?
- Do you mess up an interview, fail to complete an essential piece of work, or offend someone whose goodwill would offer you significant support?
- Do you consistently hide your talents?
- Do you dress so as to disguise your good features?
- Are you careful to avoid competitive situations?
- Do you withdraw an application when you find that a friend or sibling has applied for the same position?

Though these habits might protect you from envy, they might also prevent you from succeeding as much as your abilities allow. You might initially take one step toward overcoming your fear of success by speaking out or going ahead even when you catch sight of that urge to step back. You may learn that either no one punishes you for trying or succeeding, or that, if they do, it does not really hurt you.

Even if you reach your goals and develop your capabilities, you may experience a lingering anxiety that drains away pleasure.

- Do you expect someone to mock you or shame you after you have reached a goal or received an award?

- Do you anticipate that your success will arouse hostility in others?
- Do you deny your pride in your achievements to friends and family?
- Does your mood plummet after you experience success?

Even if you are able to pursue your goals (with rigorous modesty, hiding your light under a bushel), these habits probably mean that you do not enjoy your achievements, and that's a pity. Or perhaps you cannot enjoy your achievements because you are motivated by the desire to please someone who will never be pleased by you. When you realize that approval will never be granted, you feel drained of hope and are vulnerable to depression. Two things to keep in mind are: first, an envious mother's starting and finishing point is dissatisfaction, and you cannot change that; second, there is considerable scientific evidence that shows that pursuing the approval of others leads to greater unhappiness than pursuing what you yourself value.

A THIRD PART of the audit concerns your continuing relationship with a parent. Does your parent's envy remain an issue in your adult life?

If you still have to deal with a mother's envy, if you still confront this difficult dilemma, ask yourself whether you now have the power to challenge her, to tell her what you see, or to ignore it.

Try the one-step-at-a-time approach by testing whether you have new abilities to withstand her envy. Perhaps your mother has changed and has grown stronger and more accepting. Perhaps the power you thought you had to offend her with your achievements has diminished.

See if you can keep your nerves steady and reassure her that your achievements have not diminished her but are a credit to her.

But also consider whether the issue is still live, or whether it is the child inside you who feels threatened.

In any single moment we are responding to a mother through two forms of memory: explicit and implicit. Explicit memory includes sensory, semantic, episodic, narrative, and autobiographical memories. We can describe explicit memories. They are conscious and accessible to us. Implicit memory includes sensory, emotional, and procedural memories as well as stimulus-response conditioning. Implicit memories are not conscious, but they shape our emotional responses. When implicit memory is activated by what is happening in the present, we link its emotional impact to something that happened in the past. Words or gestures that might be neutral are perceived as threatening because we imbue them with painful memories. Because these memories are implicit, we are unaware that we are reading the present as though it were the past.

A good exercise is to reflect on whether this relational dilemma persists. Or are you still dealing with expectations based on implicit memory?

- When that familiar rush of fear or rage comes over you, pause and focus on the actual present-tense words and behavior.
- Try holding these in your mind, and perhaps even writing them down.

- Try to identify the threat they pose.
- Consider whether you remain as vulnerable as you feel.
- Try writing down past events that gave rise to similar feelings.
- Assess whether the past events really are similar to those in your contemporary life.

Gradually you will catch sight of the implicit memories that may needlessly render the present as difficult as the past. The power to assess your fears—where they stem from and whether they still apply to you—may allow you to recalibrate the fear that your success and happiness pose dangers to the people you love.

Chapter 7

THE EMOTIONALLY UNAVAILABLE MOTHER

"How much of my attention does my child need?"

"Can my child still thrive if I do other things, even when he is very young?"

"Will my child be disadvantaged if other people look after her?"

These familiar questions spring from anxieties about being a "good mother," anxieties that have wielded an ever-tightening grip on mothers over the past three-quarters of a century. Being a reliable, loving parent—a parent who provides shelter, food, discipline, and direction—is no longer thought sufficient. A parent's job is now seen as maximizing every aspect of a child's potential. Anxiety about the quality and strategies of mothering pervades our culture, fed by impossible ideals and raising unrealistic expectations.

One widespread concern is whether a child needs a full-time mother. This concern has arisen alongside increasing demands on women's commitments in the workplace. It has also arisen from multiple misinterpretations of psychological findings.

In the middle of the last century, psychologists coined the term "separation anxiety." This term describes a normal developmental phase triggered by a child's special awareness of a mother's presence and a mother's absence. At around the age of nine months, a child easily grasps the difference between a mother and other people. But he does not yet have the conceptual sophistication to realize that his mother has an existence quite separate from him. When he does not see, hear, feel, or smell his mother, he believes that she has "disappeared," that she simply ceases to exist. Until he builds that conceptual scaffold in which a person and a relationship continue even when he and she are separated, the child is overcome by terror when his mother puts him down, waves good-bye, and disappears from his sight.

Initially, separation anxiety was seen as a normal phase that would pass as a child's concept of people became more sophisticated. There was no suggestion, when this phase was first noticed, that separation from a mother harmed a child. Subsequent studies showed that prolonged separation resulted in a disturbing recalibration of a child's capacity to connect to others. When infants in the first year of life were separated from their mothers, they cried; they did not sleep; they did not eat; they became listless and dejected. Older children, too, showed marked anxiety. At first, the young child protested at the separation. Restless and tearful, he seemed to search for his mother, still hopeful that the separation would come to an end. Later, protest was replaced by despair. The child remained preoccupied with his mother and on the lookout for her, but he was more fretful and plaintive than alert and expectant. Eventually, despair gave way to detachment. The child seemed to lose hope as he adapted to a mother's absence by suppressing all emotion. There is a kind of terrible peace in a child who no longer expects to find his mother. Once this defensive apathy is adopted, it is hard to dismantle. Even when his mother returns, the child remains unresponsive, indifferent. It is as though he has lost the capacity for attachment.

The children who were observed in these stages of protest, despair, and detachment were either orphans cared for in institutions or children hospitalized and deprived of contact with a parent. Yet some psychologists interpreted these observations as evidence that a young child needs his or her mother every day, every hour of the day. They warned that without a mother's continuous presence a child would protest against the separation, then despair, and eventually detach from this bond, listless and apathetic. Repeatedly, this extrapolation has been shown to be groundless, yet the concern as to whether a mother is devoting enough time and attention to her child continues to strike fear into the heart of the family.

We have seen how a child, from birth, connects with his mother, but he is also capable of connecting with other people. The evolutionary drive to connect with others, to know and be known by other people, shows up in infants only a few days old as they scan faces and make eye contact. This highly appealing behavior engages the attention of a range of people, including those outside the family. Children learn to prefer the person who is most intricately engaged with and attuned to them. Children themselves play a part in the general conspiracy to make mothers doubt whether they are giving their child enough time and attention. Children are eager to have a mother to themselves. Nevertheless, children are built to thrive in real life, and in real life a mother is a person with a range of interests, needs, and responsibilities.

Children have evolved to thrive with ordinary human parents. In study after study, research shows that children are sturdy creatures who can accommodate a parent's human need to have a range of interests and activities, along with individual quirks and limitations. Nevertheless, extreme assessments of a child's need for a mother continue to haunt many families.

In fact, according to the evolutionary anthropologist Sarah Blaffer Hrdy, children have evolved to be "alloparented." Children are programmed to tolerate being cared for by a number of people, not only their biological parents. To care for their slow-developing and energy-consuming children, primitive humans would have required a network of mothering figures, not the sometime-isolated caregiver a mother often is today. Babies' rudimentary but finely tuned empathy, their ability to read others' intentions, their desire for connection with others, their attentiveness to others' responses and emotions, prime them to elicit care from a wide range of people—indeed, from pretty much anyone who comes into contact with them.

The anxiety-producing and guilt-enforcing cultural myth that a mother must be constantly available to her child blurs the distinctions between normal distraction and normal breaches in attention, on the one hand, and a terrifying, heart-sinking emotional absence, on the other. It is the latter—that disturbing emotional absence—that I consider in this chapter.

"Being There" and "Being Dead"

The intensity of the mother/child interaction is generally so satisfying and delightful to a child that he or she is very likely to protest at any interruption. Soon, however, the child learns that relationships continue during gaps in face-to-face contact. She gains a general, flexible concept of a person with whom a relationship is sustained; the mother is "there" for her even when they are apart. "Being there" for a child does not mean being constantly in her presence. "Being there" suggests a flow of access and interest; it suggests *capability* of focus and support. The epitome of *not* "being there" for a child is not physical absence but *emotional* absence. More chilling than coldness, more nerve-racking than anger, emotional absence deprives a child of a basic sense of self. There is no resonance, no responsiveness, no mutuality. Emotional absence produces a ghostly sense of "being there" and "being dead." The most common causes of a mother's emotional absence are drug abuse and depression.

JANE, NOW SEVENTEEN, remembers clearly her first encounter with her mother's emotional absence. At the age of about five, she was trying to climb on a chair to reach her lunchbox. She asked her mother for help and pulled at her sweater, but found her mother "staring, still, really blank." Though her mother sometimes "cries and throws things," it is more common for her to be "really calm, like she's not there, like she's just some body suit occupying space in the house." That eerie calm still frightens Jane. She tries, she says, "to turn myself into stone so I don't feel anything."

Jane's mother, Eileen, admits she is dependent on alcohol and painkillers. "Ever since, I don't know when, way back, maybe when Janie was so high"—she indicates the height of a five-year-old—"I kind of like to find this real quiet place inside me, where I don't feel too much. I need that relief. It's not really a high. Don't think I go for a high. It's just a nice quiet place." In this "quiet place" the world contracts. Thoughts are gentle, half-formed, and have no bite. As a child, Jane looked on in despair as her mother was caught up in some inner drama she could neither see nor comprehend. Her mother was physically present but emotionally disengaged.

Duncan is now thirty-seven and still carries within him his childhood experience of an emotionally absent mother.

> My mother could be sitting right next to me and all of a sudden she's far away. Not like she's thinking of something else and will snap back, but like she's buried somewhere and I can't get to her. She looks at me with those haunted eyes. . . . I still get scared and think of soul snatchers. I got in a habit of rocking in my chair and humming, and other people told me to stop it, but Mother didn't notice and I was just trying to keep time until she came back.

Duncan has learned from his grandmother and from "the little I can piece together from a lot of broken memories" that his mother was depressed from the time of his birth. "I grew up with this and was used to it, but it never felt normal. It still really hurts me, because I'd love to—you know—bring her back to life."

EMOTIONAL ABSENCE PRESENTS a child with a paradox: "I love my parent and need to be close to her, but I cannot get a response. Her inner life is either inaccessible to me or dark and distorted. I can be physically close to her, but not really close."

In this chapter we will see different ways sons and daughters adapt to this paradox as they ask: "How can I connect with a parent who is, emotionally speaking, far away? How can I know whether she is "there" or "not there"? How can I protect myself (and perhaps my siblings, or my father) from the impact of this strange absence?" A son or daughter may also wonder, "Can I save my mother? Can I nurture her back to life?"

Depression

The most common cause of a mother's emotional unavailability to a child arises from a surge of dark emotion that sucks up the normal range of delight and curiosity and responsiveness, and leaves one blank, empty, dead—but with just enough sentience to suffer a sense of loss. This condition—*depression*—is different from unhappiness. It is different from anxiety, frustration, or anger. These feelings focus on a specific problem. We are unhappy about a boss's behavior or our failure to be promoted. We are unhappy with the pressures on us or on other family members. We are unhappy about a child's performance at school. We are anxious about the outcome of an application. We are frustrated with a job in which we cannot achieve our goals. On a day-to-day basis we face problems that make us feel less than happy, but we deal with these as part of ordinary living. Episodic and focused discontent is very different from depression.

Sometimes a specific problem runs so deep that it leaves us with a generalized unhappiness. We may have a more general unhappiness about a marriage that involves recriminations and quarrels. We may find that stresses at work leave us preoccupied, irritable, unable to relax and enjoy other things. We may be so worried about our financial situation that we find it difficult to respond to others. But even this generalized unhappiness is different from depression.

The definition that comes closest to capturing the meaning of depression is mourning for a loss of one's self. Depression is a kind of psychic death; it buries curiosity, feeling, connection. Though the term "depression" is sometimes used as a synonym for sadness, it is closer to the death of all feeling. Eileen may shout and scream and cry; she may throw things and hit people; but it is in an agony of emptiness rather than an excess of feeling. More often, she is sluggish, passive, and sees no point in doing anything, even getting out of bed, getting dressed, or eating.

If you are unhappy you can imagine circumstances that would improve your mood, but if you are depressed the entire world seems so barren and bleak that you cannot imagine what an improved world would look like. At the crux of depression is the belief that your deepest self is without value, without meaning, without purpose, without real life; therefore, changing the world around you will not improve you.

A person who is depressed might look around her and see the pall she casts on others' lives, but it does not occur to her that there is anything she can offer them. What benefit would they get, she wonders, from engaging with someone as worthless and defective as she? How could they benefit from her smile, her attention, her love? Being worthless to herself, she assumes she is worthless to others. Why bother holding her child's gaze? Why bother smiling? Why should a child care what she thinks or feels? In mourning for a lost self and in the chasms of self-preoccupation, she barely registers her child's response. She cannot see that her baby is expressing delight in her touch, her voice, her face. She is slow to pick up cues that the baby wants her attention, wants to hear her speak, and wants to be held by her. She remains aloof and cautious, unable to see that anything she does has a positive effect. Others' attempts to engage her are irritating or confusing:

"I have nothing to give you because I am nothing" is the underlying assumption.

Some people struggle with depression all their lives. Some suffer depression for a period of time and then make a full recovery. A time of particular susceptibility to depression is just after the birth of a child, and this is precisely the time of a child's life in which a mother's emotional absence is most damaging.

Postpartum Depression and Its Impact on a Child

A woman may be delighted to become a mother, yet suffer postpartum depression. She may see her baby as miraculous and beautiful, but nonetheless believe there is an impenetrable barrier between her and her child. She may value her child's well-being and safety more than anything else, yet feel like a robot as she cares for him.

Women who experience postpartum depression speak of being trapped by endless demands that are both necessary and meaningless. Many speak of hiding their feelings and disguising their real selves. They speak of "wearing a mask," "putting on a front," and "showing a good face." They "act out a role" while inside they feel "dead," or they may appear to be coping but feel caught in a whirlwind of violent emotions and disorganized thoughts. They speak about two disconnected sides of motherhood: the happy public face and the very different private misery.

These paradoxical feelings are not confined to mothers who are clinically depressed. Many mothers would recognize this dual aspect of motherhood: "I no longer have control over anything" and "I no longer know who I am" describe the experience of many women. The new constraints on their freedom, the sleepless nights, and the new routines lead to turbulent changes that are difficult for any new mother to absorb. But only in about 10 percent of cases does the turbulence impede the mother's rich interaction with a child that grounds both in pleasure and delight.

"Who's a hungry baby?" and "So, you're looking at that? What's that? Is that interesting?" and "What's the matter? Why are you crying? Are you tired?" are among the many gentle queries that stimulate a child's awareness of others and capacity for self-reflection. The routine hum of connection and engagement is lost to a child whose mother is depressed. The running commentary that helps direct a child through the crowded and sometimes inchoate experiences of a new environment grinds to a halt.

When a mother is depressed, her lightning-quick sensitivity to her baby's cues is lost. The child's shiver of fear, the tremor of interest or delight, the questioning look, the gesture reaching out to touch or be held are ignored. A child is quick to notice whether he is successful in communicating his inner states. When his cues are ignored, they rapidly atrophy. He no longer bothers to express himself; he stops trying to engage others. Important research shows young children's rapid descent into despair when a mother's face becomes frozen, still, or unresponsive. A dull face, devoid of interest or pleasure, is what babies of depressed mothers experience. The baby's facial expression comes to mirror that of his depressed mother.

When a mother is depressed, a baby is less likely to exhibit that healthy range of delight, curiosity, happiness, and interest that is so easily recognizable in a contented child. When a mother is depressed, a child's expressions of sadness, anger, and distaste multiply. Even when a parent picks him up or speaks to him, he is unresponsive. The intense gaze a child usually fixes on his mother is absent. There is little depth or variety to his interaction with others.

Even when a mother recovers, the effect of her postpartum depression on a child is likely to persist. At age three, children of depressed mothers are more limited in their ability to use expressive language. At age five, children of mothers who suffered postpartum depression are significantly more likely than other children to behave in ways that a teacher assesses as in some way disturbed. They lack a healthy child's skill in encouraging others to engage with them. As a result, they are less likely to have rewarding, compensating relationships with others.

A mother's prolonged emotional absence affects the physical and chemical makeup of a child's brain. Affective sharing—emotional exchanges between mother and baby—increases brain growth and generates the crucial brain systems that help us manage our emotions, organize our thoughts, and plan our lives. Positive emotional exchanges stimulate the growth of the cortisol receptors that absorb and buffer stress hormones. Affective sharing is an essential exercise for the brain; it builds the brain strength we need to bounce back from disappointment and failure. Our ability to understand and solve the problems that arise in our social worlds emerges in playfulness between mother and baby and their mutual delight. A depressed mother may offer basic care, but her responses are slow and cumbersome; she offers less physical interaction, less skin-to-skin contact, very little playfulness, and very little delight.

At any phase of a child's life, a mother's depression wields a devastating blow to this important relationship. The ensuing dilemma can be articulated as:

- How can I adapt to an unresponsive mother so as to retain a "good" relationship with her?
- If I do not adapt to her, how do I deal with my anger, outrage, and sense of betrayal?
- Or, do I adapt by hoping that I can make her better, and thus achieve the relationship I long for?

Imitating a Depressed Mother

Adam, age fifteen, lives a double life. At school his classmates call him "the zombie." His teachers vacillate between seeing him as "stoned" or "stupid." One teacher insisted he be tested for drugs. The test indicated that he was drug-free, but the teacher's concerns remained. He was then assessed for Asperger's syndrome. Though he does not use body language when interacting with others and appears unable to engage with other people in his class, though he shows little sign of emotional or social playfulness or spontaneous emotional expressions, there was no diagnosis of any disability.

At home he is sober, controlled, and caring as he tries to contain the impact of his mother's depression on her, on him, and on his sister.

When Adam was eleven, he came home from school to find his mother, Josie, unconscious—a result of what Josie bitterly refers to as "an underdose." This put Adam on constant guard. Every day as he leaves for school he reminds Josie of the precise time he will be back home. He wants to ensure that, even if she feels very depressed, she'll focus on the specific time when her isolation will end.

Children with depressed mothers often see their role as comforter and protector. Adam is his mother's emotional companion and shares her blank emotional state. Since she cannot reflect him, he reflects her. Her narrow emotional range is his norm. Usually the parent is the "container": the person who both literally and metaphorically holds a person, keeping intact their sense of self even if they are overwhelmed by anxiety, fear, or sadness. Because his mother is unable to contain his feelings, Adam uses his mental and emotional resources to contain hers. He tries to absorb and manage her negative feelings. In this way, he hopes to keep them both safe.

Compartmentalizing Depression

A mother's depression often generates guilt in her child. This guilt can be expressed in a variety of ways. Adam believes that he would betray his mother by feeling any happiness himself. Expressing a range of emotions different from that which his mother is capable of feeling would, in his view, be wrong. Alandra, also age fifteen, however, thinks that being sad would increase her mother's "worries." She has a "home face" that fits tightly and "suits everybody in the family," but she puts on a very different face when she leaves her home.

Alandra compartmentalizes or separates her home life— where she pushes her own feelings aside—and her school life, with its interesting classes and engaging friends, its dramatic ups and downs, its challenges and worries. She has suppressed a teenager's natural urge to confront and challenge a parent. At the age of ten she would pester her mother, Eva, for attention. Even when Eva sat stock-still, blank and empty, Alandra persisted: "Look at this, Mommy" and "Can I have some of that?" and "Do you think this is right?" and "Can I watch this program?" and "Are you gonna watch it with me?" Five years later, Alandra has given up trying to engage her mother. Instead, she is quietly cheerful and bland in her mother's presence. "I'm always upbeat at home with Mom. Upbeat but not excited. I can't load her with my stuff. She needs space to deal with what's piled on her. I give her space. That's my job at home."

Damage Limitation

Young children use their own family as a measure of what is normal, however bizarre it may appear to an outsider. Even when they can see that other families seem different, they interpret what they see in light of what is familiar. Jane explains that, as a very young child, she thought her mother was like all mothers. When she saw a friend's mother laughing and smiling, she believed the woman took off her "mask" as soon as Jane left. Now, at the age of seventeen, Jane realizes that most of her friends really do have a mother who "laughs and smiles and does things with them." She tries to offer that kind of interaction to her younger sister and brother and to protect them from thinking, as she once did, that no one shares their pleasures and pains.

It is only in the past few decades that psychologists have realized how much work children do within the family. Sometimes they take on considerable household work to ease the load on a parent. Sometimes they, like Jane, take on emotional work to protect siblings from loneliness or grief or a parent's abuse. Taking on responsibility can help a child build lifelong skills, but some types of responsibility put an overwhelming burden on a child. They forgo their own needs in order to meet the needs of others. They seem mature but are able to appear composed and competent because they have foreclosed on their own opportunities for creative growth.

Fixing Things

Many people say that children live in their own world, oblivious to the feelings and needs of others. For many years developmental psychologists thought that a young child lacked a concept of other minds. Children, it was once argued, were unable to grasp that other people saw the world differently and had different interests and thoughts. New research shows a very different picture of what children know.

Children are highly sensitive to the thoughts, moods, and feelings of people who matter to them. When their mother is unhappy, they try to comfort her. When that unhappiness is profound and prolonged, they may see their life's work as making her happy.

Every conversation I have with Jackson, age thirty-three, is shaped by his belief: "If I can't make my mother happy, then I'm a failure."

Jackson has achieved many things that should be a source of pride and satisfaction. He worked his way through college and paid off all his debt. He has qualified as an accountant and is highly regarded by his coworkers. He has a number of friends and enjoys a comfortable social life. Yet his inability to "fix" his mother's depression leaves him with an overall sense of failure. This mind-set puts him at the mercy of her demands and her moods.

Depression is generally seen as a state of passive suffering, but it is often accompanied by coercion and manipulation. Jackson's mother, Alice, phones him several times a day to record the shifting patterns of her bleak moods. "You keep me alive," she tells him at the end of the call, and he feels rewarded for his efforts. But a few hours later, she feels down and demands half an hour of his time and attention as he tries to talk her up. When he is unable to contain her moods through a series of phone conversations, he cancels all evening plans to make the two-hour drive to see her. When he leaves, she is fine, but by the time he arrives home, a phone message is waiting for him with an update on her faltering condition.

Alice is so absorbed in her own suffering that she is oblivious to the constraints she puts on her son. Jackson feels responsible for managing the moods that Alice herself cannot manage. He does not accept that there is a limit to what he can reasonably do. When he tries to waylay her depression, Alice offers a brief period of gratitude followed by the plea, "I'm unhappy; make me feel better." Jackson is pinned down by the dilemma: "Either make continuous efforts to meet my (impossible) needs, or feel terrible about yourself."

Lasting Legacies

Loving, needing, and trying to heal a depressed mother leave a distinctive legacy. A son or daughter of an emotionally unavailable mother may have difficulty gauging other people's emotions. Everyday emotions may strike them as extreme because they are accustomed to a flat or negative emotional palette. Ordinary emotions may seem to them excessive, indulgent, or even alien and dangerous.

They may also have deep-seated beliefs about the role they should play in close relationships. I call these embedded beliefs operating assumptions because they set down the taken-for-granted rules according to which these children operate or behave with other people, the roles they adopt and their gauge of what is normal.

The first operating assumption is that other people's needs are more important than your own.

Many children who have lived with and loved a depressed mother come to believe that their own emotions, however positive, are alien and dangerous. Yet powerful and varied emotions tell us who we are. Emotions may be wonderful and they may be terrible, but in both cases they reveal to us our affinities, needs, and interests. When a child has fixed his or her attention on a mother whose moods are constantly painful and who demands (however implicitly) support, they may think that controlling emotions is essential to managing a relationship. They use metaphors such as "boxes" or "sealed doors" to describe their strategies for keeping feelings in check. They may be so accustomed to watching and monitoring the person they love and depend on that they acquire great skill in reading others while they minimize and even ignore their own feelings. Their operating assumption is: "My own feelings are not important, and my role in a relationship is to manage the other person's feelings."

A second operating assumption is that you always have to be the grown-up or the person in charge.

Children and teenagers who take on adult roles may appear mature and controlled, but part of them remains a helpless and frightened child. Asked to assume more responsibility than they can reasonably manage, they develop a high-functioning facade. To maintain this façade, they have to simplify their thoughts and feelings. They make a commitment to an adult identity without exploring their interests and abilities. Even in adolescence and early adulthood—a time when young people normally experiment with different personae, seek adventure, and embrace new ideals—sons and daughters who take on the role of their mother's healer deny themselves this breadth. Opting for a simple developmental path, they avoid the healthy doubt and uncertainty that accompany more challenging self-exploration. The operating assumption that they have to be the dependable adult leads to a psychological foreclosure or closing down on the opportunity for more complex development.

A third operating assumption is that other people cannot be there for you.

When a young child tries to engage with a depressed mother and constantly fails, his image of "mother" may be transformed from that of a vital presence to a pallid, inanimate, deathly figure. The extreme operating assumption that may become embedded is: "The mother I have internalized is dead." The actual mother may be alive, but the image in the child's mind is of someone as dead, cold, unyielding. The child goes through a period of mourning, first protesting against the loss, then despairing at ever regaining his mother, and finally detaching from her. His or her interactions with a mother may appear reasonably normal; but to the child, these have little meaning other than routines played out with a ghostly figure. Children who have internalized a "dead mother" often speak of other people as "shells." Other people wear "masks of emotion." They are not "really there." The child of a depressed mother may operate on the assumption that no one can really be there for them and that displays of emotion are not real. Even apparently positive exchanges may not be rewarding because the child may believe that the other person is dead inside.

Different Children, Different Responses

Experiences with a difficult mother can shape the very structure of a son's or daughter's personality; yet the impact of these experiences is not determined or fixed forever. "Difficult mother" describes a multifaceted and varied relationship; and though a mother wields enormous power, the child, too, interprets and shapes the relationship. One child may experience a depressed mother as difficult, while a sibling may form a more comfortable and rewarding relationship with the same mother.

Sometimes a mother demands more of one child—perhaps the older one, or the more pliant one, or the more capable one. Sometimes a mother favors one child over another, because of either gender, birth order, or temperament. Sometimes one child becomes a repository for a mother's resentment or dissatisfaction, or is used as the mother's scapegoat for all that is wrong in her life. But a child also influences a mother's responses. One child soothes, amuses, or rewards a mother more than another. Hence, children who share a mother may experience her very differently.

Let us suppose that two children have an unresponsive mother who suffers from long-term depression. One of those children is her grandmother's "special child." Her grandmother lavishes attention on her, praises her, takes her on outings, and engages with her interests. The other child is so withdrawn that the grandmother feels distant and diffident. This shy child senses her grandmother's unease and so seeks out her mother. She discovers that from time to time her mother's mood does lighten. Her ability to impact on her mother's moods is so rewarding that she repeatedly exercises this skill and works hard to develop it further. She sees that no one else can lift her mother's moods as successfully as she can, so she makes this her special responsibility.

Different children also have different genetic tolerances for difficult circumstances. The "orchid gene" is the name given to a variation of the gene that influences how vulnerable one is to difficult circumstances. A child who carries this gene variant will be hypervigilant to stress, while a brother or sister who does not carry this gene variant may barely notice the conditions that put their sibling on level-five alert.

Birth order and interactions with siblings can also influence a child's experience of a mother. Jane's younger brother, for example, seems unaffected by their mother because Jane protects him. She takes him into the kitchen, closes the door, and creates background noise to buffer the sounds of their mother's sobs. She bends down close to his ear and speaks softly, her tone steady and calm. Jane's role as "mini-mother" reduces the impact of his mother's depression on her brother.

Adam and his six-year-old sister, Camilla, also have very different experiences of their mother. While Adam feels responsible for managing his mother's moods, Camilla seems oblivious to them. She plays quietly beside her virtually still-faced mother, talking to herself, drawing, interacting with dolls. The television's high volume does not appear to disturb her, though she sometimes weaves snippets of conversation from the television and the accompanying noises into her game with her dolls or into the conversations she holds with herself. She utters a running commentary on what she is drawing and which colors she is choosing for which part of the picture. From time to time she turns her face to her mother and remains still and silent for several minutes. When her mother catches her fixed gaze, there is a flicker of warmth. Camilla's shoulders rise and shiver with delight, and then she goes back to her drawing. She seems to focus more on her mother's occasional and momentary responsiveness than on her dominant dark mood.

Timing is another factor in children's different experiences of their mother. Josie was hospitalized for depression soon after Adam was born, so during the earliest months of his life, when his social brain was forming, his inner states were not represented to him by a mother's responsiveness, so he missed some crucial early stimuli. Adam's ability to pick up on signs of emotion has been compromised. The flicker of a smile that delights Camilla does not register on his sluggish radar. He and his sister live in separate relational worlds with the mother they share.

Auditing the Effects of an Emotionally Unavailable Mother

The first step in conducting a personal audit is to identify your operating assumptions. These are the embedded and possibly unconsidered assumptions that you may have acquired in the course of a difficult relationship with a mother. They may continue to underpin your behavior and expectations of others and shape your interpretation of others' behavior. They can be uncovered by considering the following questions:

- Do you think that the purpose of social interactions is to regulate other people's feelings?

- What flits at the edges of your consciousness when you ask yourself whether you "should" speak up or keep quiet, whether you "should" stay in a room with someone or leave them alone, whether you "should" visit them, whether you "should" do as they ask, however inconvenient?
- Do you anxiously monitor other people's responses?
- Do you often find yourself with these worrying questions: "Will they be pleased when I give them this news?" "Will they be pleased when I do this for them?" "Will they fall apart if I forget something, fail to notice something, or decline to do as they ask?"
- Do you vacillate between hope and fear as you consider the effect you have on others?
- Do you think that your job is to notice what everyone else is feeling?

The second step is to weigh these operating assumptions against the range of your own interests and desires when you interact with your mother. "Weigh" here is used metaphorically, in the sense of what you carry around with you and whether it feels like a burden:

- Do you feel you have a choice in how to behave, or do her wishes dictate your actions again and again? (This may apply only to your mother; you may have adopted your management techniques with a difficult mother as a general strategy.)
- If you decide not to do what she asks, or what you imagine she wants, do you brood over possible punishing consequences?

- Do you focus anxiously on others' moods and emotions?
- Do you try to guess and provide what others need?

The third step is to assess how pervasive these operating assumptions are. In assessing whether they shape your identity, you could ask:

- Do I see myself as "good" insofar as I can make other people happy?
- Is it my job to watch for other people's feelings and manage these feelings for them?
- Do I panic at the thought of not being able to "fix" someone else's moods?
- Do I consider my own emotions as alien or dangerous?

Step four is to consider how much these operating assumptions dominate you:

- Does someone else's unhappiness, whether passively presented or openly expressed, take center stage in your decision-making process?
- Can you feel a sudden shift of priorities when another seems disengaged, distressed, or disturbed?
- Do you shelve your short-term, medium-term, or even long-term plans to address another person's mood?

Step five is to identify the specific behaviors guided by these operating assumptions:

- Think about various things you have done during the past several weeks or months that have been driven by the operating assumptions you have identified. These might be visits made, or gifts or invitations bestowed, or words spoken. Weigh the emotional burden of this behavior on yourself.

This audit will help you catch yourself in the act of adhering to operating assumptions that constrain you. It will help you make sense of some of your own decisions that frustrate you.

Example of a Personal Audit

Some of the case studies in this chapter involve people who are too young to conduct their own emotional audits. But if thirty-three-year-old Jackson were to engage in this exercise, his audit would begin with the question:

- Do I feel I have a choice how to behave, or do my mother's wishes dictate my actions again and again?

He could then reflect:

"My operating assumption is that if I do everything my mother asks, then she'll be happy, and I should do whatever I can to make her happy. If I don't do what she asks, my heart sinks to the floor and the anxiety stone sets in my stomach."

Bringing this operating assumption to light reveals the constraints it places on him.

Suppose he asks:

- Do I see myself as "good" insofar as I can make other people happy?

This would lead him to reflect:

"I think my role in life is the good son. Therefore, I drive to see my mother every weekend, and I expect that she'll see I'm a good son and that will make her happy. When I discover that she is not happy, I drop everything else and direct my energy to easing her pain. When these efforts have only a temporary effect, I feel like a failure. I worry that she might die and that I'll be responsible."

This links his operating assumptions to his identity.

Suppose he asks:

- Is it my job to watch for other people's feelings and manage these feelings for them?

He could then explore his motives:

"I went to see her this weekend because she sounded down and I wanted to make her happy. And this is what I generally do. I always do this for my mother. And I get very anxious when someone else asks me to do something. I don't really feel it's okay to say no. I worry that they'll collapse inside if I decline to do what they ask."

From this point in the audit, Jackson can begin to consider whether he should revise some of his operating assumptions. Of course this is not easy. A long-term anxiety that something you do or fail to do will "kill" your mother, or the worry that she may really be dead inside cannot be easily swept aside. But once the anxiety is out in the open, it can be a reference point for challenge and revision.

Balancing the Books

Some of the operating assumptions that are acquired as you manage a difficult relationship enhance empathy and interpersonal skills. Living with difficult people can make us better at understanding and negotiating with others. Some positive things we may learn from coping with a depressed mother include:

- How to be a "container" for another's unhappiness. This means you can show someone close to you that you remain intact even when they have very uncomfortable feelings. A "container" is also someone who can regulate their own moods when someone else is out of control.
- How to "read" someone, to attend to the myriad of facial movements and physical gestures that signal inner states.
- How to spot the chink in someone's low mood, and use that opening to good effect.

Of course there are many possible drawbacks to having to interact with a depressed mother, and these include:

- Discounting the importance of your own feelings.
- Feeling guilty when anyone is unhappy.
- Being unable to tolerate your own emotions.
- Foreclosing on self-exploration, growth, and confidence.

After the Audit

Changing something as deep-seated as operating assumptions involves a shift in a sense of who you are. These embedded instructions for your decisions and priorities become so much a part of you that changing your way of thinking seems impossible. "Who will I be if I no longer think about myself and relationships in these familiar ways?" you may ask. Kathryn Harrison, reflecting on her life with a difficult mother, writes, "Who would

I be without my mother? All my life I've understood myself as her child, as the child who strove to make her love me. Without her, there'd be all this . . . this room left over inside."

This "room left over inside" need not remain empty. It can be filled by new stories that make new sense of configurations in one's experience and lead to new operating assumptions— assumptions that expand and liberate us. A big step forward in creating a new story is to understand the old one.

Chapter Eight

AM I A DIFFICULT MOTHER?

The Difficulty of Being a Mother

"A M I a difficult mother?" is a question that comes as a knee-jerk reaction to any mention of "difficult mothers." This is a phrase that triggers anxiety. Some typical worries are:

"Am I doing something that might harm my child?"

"What about the time I lost my temper when my child was simply asking for another story, or a few more minutes before going to bed, or when I had a bad day at work?"

"When I slammed the bedroom door, or shouted 'Finish your dinner,' or berated him for spilling the milk he was pouring into his cereal, did I leave him with an internal monster mother, forever angry, forever critical?"

"Do my long days at work hurt my child?"

"Do the rules I set down protect or harm her?"

"Am I the best possible mother—the mother my child deserves?"

The concept of "mother" resonates with such power that mothers are often seen as wholly and solely responsible for the physical and psychological well-being of their children. Indeed, mother love in some form is essential to a child's survival. It has also been enshrined in culture. Yet a mother has a range of feelings for her child. Not all of these are positive. The outbursts of inevitable impatience fall outside the culturally approved versions of mother love. The difficulty of pursuing many of her own interests and goals as she attends to a child's needs may cast a shadow across the blissful satisfaction that a mother is expected to feel. These expectations generate impossible ideals of mother love, and some mothers feel they have to draw a mask over some of their real feelings in order to be acceptable to others.

In this chapter I address the concerns of many mothers as to whether their richly varied humanity casts them into the role of a difficult mother. I mark differences between the common experience of being overwhelmed by the difficulties of being a mother, on the one hand, and the exceptional condition of being a difficult mother, on the other. Then I consider the experiences a difficult mother may have had in her own childhood. These often generate a cycle: a mother may reproduce the difficult relationships she had as a child; and her child in turn may, as a mother, initiate a difficult relationship with her own child. In exposing the mechanisms of this reenactment, we can see ways to break the negative cycle.

Difficult Mother or Real Mother?

A human is born in a particularly helpless state, one that for other species would be considered premature. A calf can walk within hours of birth. A kitten is independent of its mother within two months of birth. Newborn primates with fur can cling to a mother and take the initiative of holding her close, but a human baby enters the world with total dependence on a care-giver. Humans require many years of care before they can even begin to function on their own. In consequence, they remain highly sensitive to any sign of abandonment or neglect.

A human baby's sole power is to elicit care from someone else. This care is necessary to their physical survival, but it pro-vides far more than this. Care is the core context for developing relationships that give birth to a sense of self. In this interactive relationship, a human infant gains the potential to reflect on his or her thoughts and feelings and to understand other people. As a mother tends her baby, both mother and baby stretch their powers to imagine, wonder at, and understand each other. The baby then builds up a model of a person with thoughts and feel-ings, communicating with other people who also have thoughts and feelings.

Throughout childhood and adolescence, what a mother says and does is magnified by her child's lens. Her words and gestures shape the internal working model a child builds and tests in this foundational relationship. This intimate history gives a mother her special power. Much of this power is positive; but, given a child's push for independence and individuality, even the power of a good-enough mother is moderated and resisted.

Much of a mother's power arises from her child's internalized image of her. In his classic and controversial novel *Portnoy's Complaint*, Philip Roth brings a comic vitality to the potent fantasy of a mother's ubiquitous power. The opening pages describe Alexander Portnoy's boyhood conviction that his mother is everywhere and is embodied in every woman of any importance. At school Alexander is convinced that his teacher is really his mother in disguise. He marvels at her ability to change shape, to change clothes, to assume different voices. Day after day he races home, amazed that she has arrived first and is sitting in the kitchen as though she had never left. He admires her magic, but he is also afraid: "I even feared that I might have to be done away with were I to catch sight of her flying in from the school to the bedroom window." The mother's image fills the boy's internal world; he sees her in every woman; she is always with him.

This powerful internal presence provides comfort but on some level it can be uncomfortable. Normally, the internal image of a mother shrinks as we grow up, but Philip Roth reminds us that even in adulthood we can be dominated by an ever-present internalized mother. This may leave us with an urge both to control her and to idealize her. A mother's love should be selfless; a mother should be fully attentive and available always. If she meets these impossible standards then her child does not have to be uneasy about his dependence. "Mother," writes Peg Streep, "is a sacred concept in our culture and has a mythology of its own." One source of this mythology is a general unease about her power.

The myth that a mother's feelings are sacred, untouched by the diversity of human rhythms, drives some women to hide behind a "mask of motherhood." One of the first writers to expose the real face behind the mask was Adrienne Rich. In her

1976 book, *Of Woman Born*, Rich bravely exposes the ambivalence, difficulty, and confusions residing within mother love: "My children cause me the most exquisite suffering of which I have any experience. It is the suffering of ambivalence: the murderous alternation between bitter resentment and raw-edged nerves, and blissful gratification and tenderness."

As so often happens when one person speaks out, other voices echo long-kept secrets. The vague shapes that once were marginalized in peripheral vision now move to the center and take on a startling clarity. Twenty years after Rich published her courageous words, Anne Roiphe wrote: "One of the reasons it's hard to express satisfaction with your life when you have children is that everywhere, every day, there is anger . . . the quick summer storm of anger, the underground anger that sometimes affects what you do or say without your even knowing it was there."

Yet sacred myths about mother love remain rooted in many cultures. In failing to meet these unrealistic ideals, a mother may worry that she is failing to be a good-enough mother. The mask goes on as she tries to feel only what she believes a mother should feel. In the powerful collection of essays *The Bitch in the House*, real mothers speak of the internal struggle with the ideals against which no one can measure up. The writing bursts the confines of sacred expectations of the selfless, ever-loving mother: "I am talking in my Mr. Rogers voice as my desperation rises," Kristin van Ogtrop writes. "Any minute now my head is going to blast off my body." In the midst of this inner explosion, she envisions "my smiling neighbors being picked up by what I imagine are calm spouses who will drive them calmly home to houses calm and collected where the children are already bathed and ready for bed." But for her "it's time to start yelling."

Having inherited from her own mother the image of a mother/child relationship that is closed off to anger and argument and which instead is managed with "kid gloves," Elissa Schappell sees her own anger as dangerous. Won't her own children flee in terror when they see her true feelings? She tries but fails to suppress the torrent of frustration that erupts when her son and daughter tease and torment each other. "These days, not only does it seem as though I am constantly shrieking in frustration, I am boggled by the banality of what I am yelling about."

Fatigue, stress, and impatience are everyday experiences of caring for children. Yet the storms of anger and the underground ambivalence often go unacknowledged because they are seen as unacceptable. Rather than protecting children from a difficult mother, these constraints may inhibit a mother's capacity to reflect broadly on her feelings, her behavior, and her child's responses.

As they measure their distance from the idealized mother, von Ogtrop and Schappell ask themselves whether they are inadequate mothers. As they describe their conundrum, however, they reveal precisely what distinguishes normal anger and ambivalence from responses that are likely to generate a difficult relational environment: insight and understanding. Von Ogtrop notes the falsehood she introduces into the relationship when she talks "in my Mr. Rogers voice." Schappell sees that her irritation at her children's bickering arises from her own stress, tiredness, and limited patience rather than from their wickedness. When her children apologize for "making" her mad, her heart melts and the comfort offered is mutual and healing. Insight into your own behavior and your child's responses offers the strongest possible protection against being a difficult mother.

Crucial Differences: Insight or Ignorance

We are normally intelligent observers of those who matter to us. Our survival, comfort, and social stability depend on our ability to anticipate how what we say and do will affect others. We try to understand why people respond to us as they do. We don't always get things right. We might walk away from a meeting thinking we have made our point and said just the right things, and then discover we have offended a colleague who heard a very different message from the one we meant to convey. When something goes wrong we are much quicker to see how someone else made a mistake than to identify our own error. But in a close relationship we have endless opportunities to refine our understanding. The key task of mother and child is to get to know each other, to anticipate and influence each other's needs and actions. Mothers tend to be so engaged with their child that they have a hard time not being swayed by the child's feelings. A difficult mother has to work hard to sustain her lack of insight. She stands guard over the closed story she tells herself and imparts to her child. She locks the door against possible adjustments and moves further and further away from a reality that can be tested.

What distinguishes good-enough mothers from difficult mothers is the good-enough mother's ability to reflect on her own anger, impatience, and ambivalence. Reflection requires a willingness to change perspective, to moderate your own needs in relation to others. It means having the imagination see how another person might respond to what you say and do. It means seeing the legitimacy of even negative responses to you. It means picking up cues about your child's feelings and thoughts even when these differ from what you expect or what you want.

One of the most pervasive characteristics of a difficult mother is a mental rigidity in clinging to her own initial perspective. This is combined with a slippery agility in keeping insight at bay. This combination of bias and cleverness is extremely confusing.

Common Tactics for Maintaining Lack of Insight

Some standard tactics a difficult mother uses to sustain lack of insight and to close off her perspective from others' include:

Ownership of the story, often in the form: "A parent knows what's right. Children need to be told what's what by someone who knows." In this mind-set the child's own knowledge and feelings are marginalized.

Discounting a child's experience: Closely related to owning the story is the global message, "You have no idea what you're talking about." The message is that there is no reason to consider a child's viewpoint because children get things wrong, have imperfect memories, and make things up. The parent is the only one who really knows anything.

Claiming high status, often in the form: "I deserve better treatment than this" or "You should show me more respect!" In this way, a child's efforts to present his or her own perspective are seen as a punishable offense. The issue remains fixed on what the child owes his or her mother.

Blaming the child for the parent's behavior: "You made me angry. Are you satisfied? You say you don't like me to shout, but you make me shout." This justifies outbursts of anger, even abusive anger. The child, not the parent, is seen to be responsible for a mother's anger.

Self-pity: A child's complaint is countered by some version of "But what about me?" A parent signals that there is a hierarchy for empathy and understanding, and that she comes first.

Denial by comparison: Related to self-pity is a competition for greater suffering. "You have no idea what I had to go through" implies that a child has no right to complain about or try to adjust the relationship because his or her mother had a more difficult time with her own mother.

Global criticism: A child who is "touched by the devil" or who has a "nasty streak" or who is "spoiled rotten" has no grounds for asking his or her views to be heard.

Criticism masked as concern, often by indicating that a child's behavior is a sign of illness: "Are you feeling better?" may be addressed to a child whenever he or she strays beyond the narrow confines of a mother's will. Sympathy replaces conversation. This tactic may be used to suggest that any negative feelings are unacceptable; discontent or just simple difference is seen as a symptom of illness.

Bland denial of the obvious: Statements such as "I wouldn't dream of preventing you from doing what you want to do" and "You know you can tell me anything" may have no connection to a mother's actual behavior.

Apparent agreement without engagement: Responding to what a child says with "Mmm, yes, mmm-hmm" gives the appearance of listening but offers no real engagement. Lack of focus, evading a point, dropping a subject, responding with off-the-point issues and comments are other common ways of offering a surface response that lacks substance.

Empty forecasts: These include apparent agreement with the promise, "I'll make things up to you." A different empty forecast might be, "You'll thank me when you're older"—a claim that a child cannot counter.

Anxious deflection: When an issue is raised that jars a parent's perspective, she may use anxiety as a deflection. It is as though an atomizer has been pressed; the room fills with stinging droplets of anxiety that infect everyone present. The child either flees from or tries to soothe the parent's anxiety.

Outright denial, for example: "I never said that" or "No one in this family is an alcoholic" or "No one ever hurt you." Sometimes denial is enforced with authority, for example: "No one in this family is allowed to speak like that."

Mockery and derision: These are harsh weapons, able to disarm a child's belief that he or she has a right to speak up. "Who do you think you are?" and "You think you're so smart" and "Take a look at yourself; who are you to tell me anything?" are likely to freeze a child's efforts to negotiate the relationship that he or she needs.

The Aikido approach: This term is taken from the martial art of using an opponent's force against the opponent. In conversation it involves taking someone's words and using them as a weapon against the person who speaks them. If a child expresses desire or criticism or need, a parent who uses the Aikido approach might use that to "prove" that a child is "naughty" or "bad." Repeated use of this approach—having your own words used against you, particularly to show that you are in the wrong—discourages openness and can put an end to the parent/child conversation.

The Difficult Mother as a Child

When I spoke to mothers who were described by their sons or daughters as difficult, I often had trouble sustaining a conversation about their own childhood experiences. Either they could not focus on a specific point or event or they fixated on a few incidents they would describe repeatedly, in similar and limited terms. Sometimes their stories about who said or did what contained inconsistent claims and unsupported accusations. Their reflections were vague and full of generalities, as though their childhood had been without clarity or detail. When I pressed for specific details about their past lives, the timelines were unclear and they had trouble putting events in order. Their stories were difficult to follow. They might mention a parent, an uncle, or a sibling and then mix up the names. They might stop in midsentence and puzzle over what they had been saying or ask again what the question was that they were trying to answer. Sentences were often left dangling, thoughts unfinished. Sometimes they talked a great deal, but the conversation looped and skirted around things, as though words were a way of obscuring communication. When I asked them to consider their son's or daughter's childhood experiences, they tended to dismiss the possibility that their own child might have been unhappy.

So, I wondered, had they themselves had a difficult mother? Had someone thwarted in them the natural-born need to make sense of their lives? Did their own childhood experiences impact on their ability to respond to their own children?

All parents were once children themselves. As children, they would have reached out to a mother for responsiveness, comfort, and connection. If she had disappointed them, if their needs had been ignored, if they had met with criticism and contempt, then surely they would try to do better by their own children? Most people who have experienced a difficult parent want to offer their child more love, better understanding, stronger support than they themselves had; but the outcome may well be that the parent who, as a child, dealt with a difficult parent will become a difficult parent herself.

There is an eerie, disturbing tendency to repeat difficulties we have experienced as children and to replicate past relationships that we found uncomfortable. Someone with an alcoholic and abusive parent may seek refuge in a friend or partner, only to discover that the most difficult aspects of her family life are reproduced in this new connection. Over and over again psychologists observe that people reproduce the patterns of relationships they are trying to escape. All too often, children who experience a difficult relationship with their parents inflict the same relationship on their children. However determined they may be to protect their child from the difficulties they experienced, they may find a parent's angry or controlling words coming out of their own mouth.

Ghosts of past relationships live within us. In her illuminating article "Ghosts in the Nursery," Selma Fraiberg describes the ways these are passed on from generation to generation. Every child is visited by "the unremembered past of the parent" and relives many of the same difficulties. Fraiberg describes a five-month-old boy who was neither growing nor putting on weight. His facial expression was grim. His body was rigid. He was withdrawn and showed a disturbing "independence" by pushing himself up toward the feeding bottle without any of the typical signs of need and pleading that infants normally display. Turning her attention to the baby's mother, Fraiberg noted that she appeared unaffected by her baby's wails, even as they continued to pierce all other listeners' ears. Then Fraiberg heard something strange in those cries. The wails were unmodulated by any of the usual rhythms of urgency and hope. His mother kept her baby clean and she kept him warm and she fed him, but those apparently joyless tasks were routinely preceded by a weary sigh.

Eventually Fraiberg uncovered the context of the mother's depression. She herself had been neglected and abandoned as a child. She had not experienced the mutual rush of pleasure in "eye love." She had not felt a mother's responsiveness to her distress or delight. In her infancy, there was no point in seeking out her mother's gaze. Now, as she interacted with her own child, the buried and painful memories were awakened. Overwhelmed by the negative feelings these memories evoked, she was unable to respond to her infant.

Unseen, unacknowledged memories are powerful, particularly

when they are painful. These ghostly presences pervade our emotions and direct our behavior. As Freud noted: "A thing which has not been understood inevitably reappears; like an unlaid ghost, it cannot rest until the mystery has been resolved and the spell broken." It is not the mother's past suffering in and of itself that locks her into a cycle of repetition, but her failure to understand and grasp the meaning of her past suffering. Fraiberg found that resolving the mystery—identifying and understanding her own suffering—could break the spell of that ghost and allow the mother to see her child with a fresh pair of eyes and learn a new repertoire of responses.

Repeating Patterns of Love

Every mother/child pair has a unique relationship, but within this endless individual variety some basic patterns of mother/child attachment can be seen. Secure attachments, for example, offer a sense of stability and safety, and these are found in approximately two-thirds of mother/child relationships. Insecure attachments characterize the remaining one-third of mother/child relationships, with approximately 8 to 10 percent being anxious attachments, in which a child is confused about a mismatch between a parent's displays of affection and a real engagement. A child who experiences this type of double bind, or contradictory messaging, may feel anxious because it seems impossible to grasp what is really going on. In an ambivalent attachment, a mother vacillates inexplicably from being loving and tender to being angry and threatening. Faced with this unpredictable inconsistency, a child tries to appease the mother, anxious to control and monitor her shifting moods.

If inconsistencies abound, then the attachment is likely to be assessed as "insecure disorganized."

What has concerned many psychologists over the years is how patterns of attachment seem to be passed down from grandmother to mother to child. A woman says in all sincerity, "I want to be more loving, more open, more reliable for my child than my mother was for me." Yet it is difficult to map out new relational pathways. Even when a woman vows to be different from her mother, she may reenact the familiar and difficult model of mothering she experienced. A breakthrough in understanding the process of this ghostly inheritance was achieved by Mary Main, who designed a series of questions and probes that shed light on mothers' own early attachment experiences. Those who themselves had secure attachments had a much easier time establishing a similarly healthy attachment with their child. Those who seemed ambivalent or detached indicated that they had experienced similarly troubled relationships with their mothers.

Memories affect us long after we think they are forgotten. They can be evoked within a powerful "remembering context" so that even as we try to make a fresh start, our behavior is shaped by the ghosts that we have not yet put to rest.

Ghostly Memories

Caring for a baby is an intimate, emotive process. The ordinary acts of holding and feeding evoke a flow of memories about your own experience of being mothered. Spontaneously, unconsciously, you draw on a repertoire of feelings and behavior that may not have been relevant to anything else since your own infancy. "This new remembering context," writes Daniel Stern, "is the raw material for an important part of the mother's reorganization of her identity as daughter and as mother. And in this remembering context, the old schemas of being-with-mother will tumble out and pervade the new mother's experience."

When experiences are painful, when they remain unseen and unacknowledged, they become ghosts that arise in the mother/child bond. A trauma your mother experienced before you were born, about which she remained silent, can nonetheless shape her response to you and hence be felt by you. In one case study, a man suffered constant anxiety; the world appeared him as a fearful place, and he was constantly on the alert for brutal attacks—although nothing in his own experiences explained this. His inability to control his fear strongly suggested that his brain had been exposed to abnormally high levels of stress hormones and that he had lower-than-normal levels of receptors for those stress chemicals. Yet as far as he or anyone else could determine, he had never experienced any kind of trauma.

Louis Cozolino, the psychoanalyst in charge of this clinical case, learned from the man's mother that she had been a child during the Holocaust and had witnessed her entire family being taken away by the Gestapo. She never spoke about her past experiences of separation or the difficult terms of her survival, but this trauma left her ever alert to disaster. She believed she was protecting her son by silencing her traumatic history; but she, like most of us, greatly underestimated the amount of information about herself and her past that she communicated to her child. The ghosts of our past can persist for generations, particularly those ghosts that have not been named.

But memory, however traumatic, does not fix behavior in stone. Mothers themselves undergo change and growth. Often they change and grow in response to their child. Relationships are mutually created. The mother's remembering context may initially trigger anxiety and ambivalence, but children have evolved to be, as Sarah Blaffer Hrdy says, "activists and salesmen, agents negotiating their own survival." From birth they are notoriously good at charming their caregivers, flattering them by following them with their adoring gaze, responding to voice and touch. They are also good at making demands. Their cries are at the exact pitch to goad anyone with a human ear to soothe and coax them into silence. Babies are also skilled at choreographing interactions, every one of which is a building block in the relationship. A woman who begins the complex activities of mothering with a disturbed remembering context may falter initially. The ghosts of her past impede the rhythmic flow of the mindbuilding dance with her child, but her child may be an excellent teacher, whose interactive lessons soon result in a confident, responsive mother.

Many mothers who themselves experienced deprivation, abandonment, brutality, and abuse go on to form a strong and comfortable relationship with their child. Negative cycles can be replaced by a virtuous cycle of positive attachment, as the mother/baby conversation takes precedence over the remembered patterns of interaction. The key to breaking the negative cycle is not to banish the remembering context but to use memory to reflect on and revise responses. The mother Selma Fraiberg described, who sat passively when her baby cried, whose face drained of emotion as her five-month-old son's face reddened with rage, lacked a bodily memory of caring and comforting. Self-absorbed, dreamlike, distant, she simply did not know how to engage with a baby. But as she uncovered the painful memories of her own neglect, she could see what she had to learn anew, without the bodily memory to guide her. Ghosts in the nursery, Fraiberg concludes, do not perpetuate "blind repetition of their morbid past." If a woman can speak coherently about her experiences and reflect on her dislocation and longing, she can then see what injured her. She can then protect her child from similar emotional harm.

Difficult Mothers Do Not Learn

Learning new ways to develop and maintain relationships is always possible. The common saying, "You can't teach old dogs new tricks," is both false and dangerous. Early experiences wield enormous influence, but we can change our perspective and establish new habits. We can literally change our minds as the power to observe, assess, and reconsider rewires the circuits in our brain.

Mothers who generate a difficult relational environment are unlikely to consider different possible interpretations of their behavior. They are unlikely to see things from a child's point of view or to accept that their actions have an effect different from the one they intend. They barrel ahead with incandescent self-righteousness, affronted by any effort to adjust their perspective. In this mind-set, they are likely to interpret their child's efforts to be "activists and salesmen, agents negotiating their own survival" as signs of hostility, perversity, or in some extreme cases evil.

Of course, mothers can grow and learn. "Difficult" is not necessarily a constant characteristic. The woman in Fraiberg's clinic who sat passively when her baby cried, who "cared" for her child without joy, subsequently—after Fraiberg's clinical intervention—became an engaged, responsive parent. Most people can improve their abilities to respond and to "listen" (in the broadest sense), either through clinical interventions or through their own efforts. In general, mothers who had difficult attachment experiences but who were able to remember them, reflect on them, and understand how they had been hurt by them were able to use these negative experiences to deepen their awareness of what could hurt and hinder their child.

Mentalizing—the ability to identify and reflect on thoughts and feelings, both one's own and other's—plays a key role in early learning and attachment, but it is also an essential tool throughout the life span. At any time in a child's life, a mother's understanding, appreciation, and responsiveness are likely to have a welcome impact. As we improve our ability to mentalize, we see the complexity of interactions. This ability can set in motion a very different cycle of mothering.

Conducting Your Personal Audit

Are you at risk of reproducing your difficult experiences for your child?
If you had a difficult relationship with your mother, you may be determined to be a very different type of mother, yet you are probably anxious and uncertain as to whether you can achieve this. The first step is to reflect on your own family experiences.

WRITE YOUR OWN FAMILY STORY.
- Describe your parents during your childhood.
    Give specific examples to illustrate the general terms you use. (If you say it was all awful, or pretty normal, give examples that show this.)

- Check whether there is a good fit between your general comments and the specific episodes and examples you provide.

  You want to look for a good fit between generalities and specific memories. If there is a good fit, then your story is likely to be coherent and you are at lower risk of reproducing your own difficult experiences in your child.

- Write down a list of adjectives that describe your relationship with each parent. Then set out memories of specific events, actions, or words to support these adjectives.

- Look over what you have written. Can you explain why your parent or parents acted as they did?

- Now describe your current relationship with your parents. Can you see how this has changed over time?

- Test your ability to shift perspective by writing about the same events from different people's viewpoints. Check that what you write has a clear and consistent timeline.

- Finally, consider how your childhood experiences have affected your current behavior, particularly your behavior as a parent.

It is not the answers to these questions that matter as much as engaging with them and exercising your ability to reflect, expand, and revise.

Auditing Your Defenses

The next step is to consider a list of common defenses and to reflect on whether you revert to these by force of habit.

DO YOU TRY TO "OWN" YOUR CHILD'S STORY?

A child's version of his or her experiences, whether they occurred yesterday or years ago, can amaze a parent. You may recognize some elements but disagree with your child's interpretation of what was going on if many details seem wrong:

- Do you respond with, "Nonsense"?
- Or do you consider your child's view and show a willingness to learn?
- Do you insist that your child's memory is faulty, or are you willing to question your own memory?

Denying outright the validity of a child's memory can be a way of taking control of a child's story and therefore refusing to listen. In an intimate relationship, not listening is painful and offensive.

ARE YOU QUICK TO BLAME YOUR CHILD WHEN YOU
FEEL ANGRY?

- When you "lose it," do you blame your child for "making" you shout and fume, or do you see how your anger may inflict pain on your child?
- Do you feel "he deserves to suffer," or are you able to see

that your reactions come from within you, that they are not the fault of someone else?

WHEN YOUR CHILD MAKES A MISTAKE, DO YOU SEE THAT AS A GENERAL CHARACTER FLAW?

- When your child behaves badly, do you see this behavior as representative of who she is, or do you see it as a specific problem?

Global criticism can open the wellspring of shame, but specific criticism is often appropriate and constructive. Sometimes people adopt styles of criticism they experienced from their own parents and use these even when they were hurt and frustrated by them. You may have to take deliberate steps to form new habits.

Your first reaction may be to blame the child. Perhaps you link this mistake to others and see your child's general lack of judgement. Perhaps you react to the situation solely according to the strength of your current feelings.

This reaction can be moderated with insight: You see your child's mistake and you are angry, but you could call to mind the child's perspective. Instead of venting your own anger, you then learn to consider how to convey to your child the specific problem in his or her behavior.

DO CRITICISM AND COMPLAINTS INVARIABLY MAKE YOU TOO ANGRY TO REFLECT WHETHER THEY ARE JUSTIFIED?

- Can you hear complaints and criticism from your child without becoming enraged? Do you fling criticism and complaints back, or can you reflect, listen, and explore?

- Are you able to sustain focus on your child's problems or your child's frustrations without punishing him by ridiculing his complaints or accusing him of disrespect?

Posing these questions to yourself may be uncomfortable; but if you can reflect on your own behavior and be alert to a child's response, you are likely to replace the defenses that generate a difficult relationship with responses that aid attentiveness and understanding.

The Earliest Stages of Parenting

In the very early stages of parenting, the remembering context that shapes responses to a child is usually unconscious. The care you experienced, or the lack of a good model for tending an infant, are deep-seated but not irreparable. If you feel that your own experience of early care was deficient, your implicit memories may be the root cause. You may make a special effort to:

- Hold your baby so that he or she can see your face.
- Follow your baby's gaze.
- Mimic your baby's facial movements.

    If you think your baby is trying to smile, smile back and show pleasure. If your baby is crying, focus on her quietly for a moment, vocalize your concern, and use your face to express (contained) discomfort.

    Observe how your baby responds to your facial movements.
- Try making distinctive movements with your mouth and see how she imitates you. If you stick out your tongue, you are likely to see even a three-week-old baby work to do the same. This shows how carefully she is watching you, how intent she is to learn from you.

- Modulate your voice in different ways while you are holding your baby. See if you can sense the baby's physical responses (either in the movement of her arms and legs or in the direction of her gaze) to your different vocal tones.
- Watch your baby watching you. Hold the baby's gaze and see how her gaze follows yours. Use that "eye love" to show appreciation for her attention.
- When your baby starts to fuss and fret and turn her head away, you can break off the eye contact, let her have a rest from this exciting interaction, and wait for your baby to give cues that she is ready to reengage with you.

If you find you are doing this quite naturally, then you may have had sufficient good experience of care when you were a baby, however difficult you felt your relationship later became.

Mentalizing: Different Meanings for Different Ages

Children cherish a parent's attention at most stages of their lives. They want to be known and understood. Failure to "see," to understand, and to listen in this powerful relationship strikes a child as a moral failing and a betrayal of the parent/child bond. Your child is likely to be your best teacher for lessons in attentiveness. However, below are some common behaviors that a child is likely to find in a difficult parent:

- Switching off when a child talks about his unhappiness.
- Telling a child he is wrong to feel as he does.
- Thinking that, if he is upset with the parent, then there is something wrong with him.
- Seeing only what it suits the parent to see.

- Assuming a child cannot have feelings and thoughts that are different from the parent's.
- Assuming the parent knows precisely what the child thinks and feels.
- Shutting out the child's messages.
- Hearing what the child says about himself as a criticism of the parent.

Sons and daughters seek out "real" mothers, not perfect mothers. In doing so, they will inevitably experience some frustration and disappointment; but, as the psychoanalyst Alice Miller reflects, "Every life and every childhood is filled with frustrations; we cannot imagine it differently; it is not the suffering caused by frustration that does damage, but being forbidden by the parent to articulate and express the suffering."

Chapter Nine

RESILIENCE: OVERCOMING A DIFFICULT MOTHER'S POWER

The Inner Paradox

W<small>E DEVELOP</small> a sense of self not only through our inner feelings and sensations but also through our relationships with others. Mother and baby form what is called the "foundational relationship" in which our mother stimulates our rudimentary concept of "I" and "other." Through our mother's curiosity about our experiences and emotions, we become self-aware. A prolonged difficult relationship with our mother is likely to impact on how we interpret our own inner world.

Understanding who we are and making sense of our own stories are vital parts of our well-being. Making sense of our important relationships is integral to making sense of ourselves. This is a physical and emotional as well as an intellectual exercise.

Our thoughts about the big things in our lives summon up strong physical sensations. Feelings infuse our view of the world. When our positive experiences are broadly in sync with our expectations, when we feel we are making ourselves clear to others, when we understand what is said and how another person's actions fit into the conversational flow, we feel whole, confident, and energized. When we are mystified by shifting moods and inexplicable motives from someone we love or need, we cannot find our footing; we get emotionally seasick.

Children depend on a mother's genuine willingness to understand them. A difficult mother takes ownership of her child's own stories or autobiographical self. She condemns, limits, and distorts them. Instead of checking her expectations and demands against the child's own desires and abilities, she tells him who he is or who he should be. This presents a dilemma: Forgo your own voice—the link between your inner and outer self—and maintain this significant relationship, or try to maintain your own voice but suffer contempt, criticism, and ridicule from someone you depend on.

If you ignore your own thoughts and deny your own wishes in order to comply with a difficult mother's demands, then you are left to develop a false self. If you keep faith with your own feelings, thoughts, and needs, then you are denied a genuine relationship with someone you love.

There is a fatal problem with either option. Even when you are willing to forgo your own voice, you cannot comply with the terms of this dilemma. An enormous amount of mental energy is used in the effort to repress what you think and feel. Your real thoughts and feelings fight back and seek some route to expression. You are probably punished for the partial expressions of your thoughts and feelings. Without resonance from the people you love, you only half understand yourself. When you speak out, and experience dissonance, you begin to doubt the value of what you want to say.

Most mothers collaborate with their child's natural-born pursuit of human understanding. They sift and separate their own needs from those of their child. They learn about a child by watching and listening and questioning. They show they are an attentive listener even in the role of guide and disciplinarian.

In a good-enough environment children work hard to teach their mother how to be a good-enough parent *for them*. In different ways, at different stages in their lives, sons and daughters use different tactics to update their mother on their changing views and desires. They persuade her to adjust her view of who they are and who they want to be. Persuasion comes in many forms. Sometimes a sharp "identity reminder" is enough to do the trick. "That's not what I think!" or "I haven't liked that since I was little!" Heated arguments may erupt out of a child's frustration, which may be based as much on the child's own uncertainties as on a mother's obtuseness. Adjusting and negotiating this relationship is a passionate enterprise, and it seldom avoids some cuts and thrusts. During this process there can be pitfalls and there can be tragedies. Goodwill is not always sufficient to recalibrate the relationship, and clinical records of profound and persistent misunderstanding are plentiful.

Sons and daughters who describe a difficult mother experience repeated frustration as they try to improve and renegotiate this foundational bond. They feel that their efforts to communicate, explain, and update the relationship are seen as "bad" or "wrong." They describe a mother who punishes any resistance to her control. They then feel trapped by her self-justification. The child's world becomes hazy, paradoxical, and capricious.

In the teenage years, as a son or daughter uses new powers of argument and persuasion to explain and defend themselves, a difficult mother sees her child's independence and difference as dangerous. She punishes and ridicules and ignores him. Conversations hit a brick wall or veer off course. There are deft evasions, bland obfuscations, and bizarre excuses. A child's heartfelt words seem to dissolve in chaos.

A difficult mother takes control of the personal history records, including the child's own store of memory. The message is: "As a mere child, you must be the one who misremembers; if your memories clash with my story, then you are making them up, willfully distorting them, or imagining things—as children do." The enormous emotional impact on a child of punishment or ridicule is discounted. The message is: "You have nothing to complain about." Even violent or abusive events are sometimes discounted or denied or redacted by the very people we depend on to resonate with our inner lives. A difficult mother presents us with the paradox of being close but being closed to us.

Trying to Understand

The psychologist Bruno Bettleheim said that most things are bearable if we can make sense of them. Some sons and daughters of difficult mothers expend enormous energy trying to make sense of their mother's behavior. They ponder over questions such as "Why does she get so angry?" and "Why were my own needs irrelevant?"

Some try to enlist their mother's help in clarifying their story. Even in adulthood they may feel that their own perspective lacks depth and validity unless their mother accepts their version. But acceptance is unlikely: by definition a difficult mother is not an emotional listener. She is unwilling to adjust her own perspective in response to her child's. A difficult mother does not collaborate with her child's efforts to clarify and consolidate their story. Instead, she sticks rigidly to her own story. A request to revise that story is often seen as a personal attack. In retaliation, a difficult mother may reinforce the dilemma between a child claiming his own knowledge and needs, on the one hand, and being frozen out by her, on the other.

Many children then develop strategies to cope with this dilemma. They try to comply with the mother's views and deny their own. Others opt to conceal themselves, appearing to comply to the mother's expectations while secretly trying to know themselves. Some children are able to draw on other resources and establish close relationships that supply what their foundational bond lacks. "This is what my mother demands, but I've learned that I can have broader, more genuine relationships with others," they discover. Grandparents, siblings, teachers, and friends, are all possible resources for emotional support. Even in circumstances of severe difficulty, some children are able to draw other people into a relationship with them. They take note of who might be responsive; they learn how to engage others in their lives; and they build a relationship with them. This process of engaging with others boosts their confidence, and the positive effects multiply.

The day-to-day impact of a difficult relationship may ease as sons and daughters grow, share problems with friends, receive love from other people, discover new ways to test and express themselves, and develop the confidence to understand themselves and others. Yet rarely are adult sons and daughters completely free from the old paradox and dilemma.

Over time, the balance of power may shift. In adulthood, a son or daughter may have the agility to move beyond the reach of a difficult mother' dilemma. An elderly mother's dependence may lead to new perspectives and appreciation for both the mother and her adult child. For some, however, the difficult relationship carries on unchanged and unabated. Even when the relationship improves in adulthood, the childhood struggles continue. A mother's death does not necessarily diminish her power. Death ends a mother's life, but not the internal models of thoughts, feelings, and expectations that a child develops in this foundational relationship.

Overcoming a Difficult Mother's Power

So what does help us overcome the power of a difficult mother's legacy?

Making sense of the relationship helps us overcome its power. Matching up our core self and our autobiographical self frees us from a mother's incoherent and ill-fitting views. When we do this with openness, with empathy for ourselves (both our past and present selves), and with a broad enough perspective, we have a good chance at recovery from that sick-making sensation of seeing ourselves as in the wrong for being unable to meet paradoxical demands.

Does understanding, with perspective and reflectiveness, really have such power?

Yes.

By making sense of childhood experiences, we can transform an incoherent relationship into a dynamic one we can reflect on and manage. Understanding alters expectations, associations, and interpretations. It changes our brains, even at the level of neuron activity and synaptic connection. By revising the stories we tell ourselves about who we are and what life has in store for us, we can develop new impulses and gut responses. The way we make sense—the way we think and rethink our lives, how we grasp and retain meaning over time—shapes the way we think. The stories that form our autobiographical self can rewire our brains.

Proof of the Power of Stories

The healing power of improved personal stories is well established. A key study shows how the complexity and coherence of their life stories protect children and teenagers from the profound disruption and disturbance of a difficult mother.

The young people in this seminal study led by Stuart Hauser were not merely unhappy; they were delinquent, uncontrolled, and a danger either to themselves or to others. Eventually, for different reasons, each was confined to a locked ward of a residential psychiatric hospital. Their rates of recovery were not good: twelve years after hospitalization, 58 of the 67 former patients still lived disturbed and unhappy lives. In searching for understanding of the young people's difficulties, the researchers had no difficulty identifying events and relationships in these young people's lives that contributed to their problems. Their home life was generally chaotic and threatening. There were few strong family bonds from which they might have drawn support to compensate for a poor relationship with the mother. There was little systematic discipline—though there was plenty of argument and abuse. Their schools lacked the resources to stimulate or control them. Their communities were either fragmented or hostile to them. However, instead of sticking with the question "Why are these young people so disturbed?" the researchers focused on the young people who recovered. They asked, "Why did nine children become successful and optimistic and trusting adults?"

Most explanations of human behavior involve, in some broad way, family influence and the genes one is born with. These two influences—nurture and nature—are no longer seen as separate factors; instead, each interacts intimately and intricately with the other. It is the environment that influences whether certain genes are active or dormant. Genes influence behavior, which in turn influences how people select and shape their environment. Then this selected environment either triggers or suppresses further genetic expression. Undoubtedly, every child in this study carried genes that made him or her vulnerable to psychological distress. They also experienced difficult environments. There was nothing puzzling about their susceptibility to breakdown and depression. But why were some of these young people able to recover? The mystery lay in their resilience.

Resilience does not mean that you no longer feel pain and disappointment. It does not mean that you are unaffected by your past. It means that you are not dominated by these difficulties. It means that you manage to avoid that disturbing cycle whereby you reproduce the behavior and the relationships that injured you. It also means that you can reflect on the patterns, the defenses, and the compromises that you developed to deal with a difficult mother. It means that you can develop more positive ways of managing your needs.

The psychologists conducting the study realized that they had many conceptual tools for assessing symptoms of disturbance but very few for assessing resilience. They described themselves as learning to "see in the dark" as they tried to understand what helped these young people recover. How could they describe in

any precise way the words, actions, and thoughts that might signal recovery?

They decided to go back to that old staple of the psychologist's
toolbox: listening. They listened carefully to the stories of the
young people who recovered and compared their stories to those
of the young people with more typical outcomes. The researchers
were hard-nosed developmental psychologists interested in science and proof. They admitted that they would not ordinarily
have put much store in any kind of talking cure; but they came to
recognize the personal narratives as a resource and a tool, a way
of creating and maintaining meaning over time. They analyzed
the interviews of sixteen young people—the nine resilient ones
and seven in the contrasting group—and noted how these young
people, with their difficult families, their experiences of disruption and loss, spoke about change, about relationships, and about
their developing ideas of themselves.

The researchers listened to the personal stories—very much
like the case histories here—without being sure what they were
looking for. As they listened, they noted important differences.
They found that those who were able to process difficult experiences had richer and smoother narratives, or stories, about their
interpersonal lives. The researchers came to realize that the significant questions to ask were:

- Do you stick to generalizations, or can you see nuance
  within a situation?
- Are your stories flexible and inclusive, or closed and
  static?
- Do you welcome opportunities for change, or resist them?
- Can you sustain relationships with other people, or do
  you reject and feel threatened by others?

- Can you focus on emotionally taxing experiences with-out vagueness, avoidance, confusion, or changing the subject?
- Do you see yourself as a force in the plotline, or as a bystander?

The young people who were still struggling in their lives told stories that were structurally simple, flat, and disorganized. They could not shift or broaden their perspective; their descriptions of themselves and their circumstances were one-sided and fixed. The researchers described them as "low density narrators." Their stories faded out when they were asked why they did something or when they were asked to describe what they generally do when things don't go well. They had little awareness of the emotions of others, and in fact seemed disconnected from their own feel-ings. When they became confused, they grew angry and "acted out." They were likely to foment trouble as a means of distracting themselves from what they could not understand.

In stark contrast, the stories of the resilient young people were complex, vivid, and clear. They did not always begin with complex, broad, or coherent narratives, but they could shift and refine their views. Here is Rachel dealing with a formulaic account of her family and then working to locate problems: "It's more or less like a family—but not really—just like in a family setup—sort of." Then she begins to identify a lacuna: "They're upset, but you know, I don't really know how they feel if they don't say anything; it's just that they get mad." And here is Pete, working toward putting others' responses in the context of his assumptions about them: "If you only feel safe when people are scared of you, they might not want to hang around. But if they aren't scared of you, then maybe you don't want to hang around."

At the age of fourteen, Pete, who once stole a gun and brought it to school, now reflects on and corrects past views about what he would gain from frightening other people. As he articulates his assumptions, previously buried in a mass of anxiety and anger, he can consider alternative ways of being with people.

There is nothing easy or predictable in the strategies of young people who recover after deeply troubled experiences. They demonstrate resilience only after a trial-and-error process. During this process many suffer setbacks; but, unlike those who remain stuck, the resilient group learned from their setbacks. They absorbed lessons in day-to-day psychology: they tried to manage their own actions so that they would not push others away. They tried to control their own feelings and to assess whether their responses to others made sense. Eventually they exercised their power to influence their own environment; they were able to leave threatening situations, to lower the emotional temperature of an argument, and to respond positively to positive behavior in other people. With these skills they were able to build up supportive relationships.

Stories, whether from folktales or fiction or theater, have power; they help to bring order to our experiences; they may introduce new themes of thought and broaden perspective. The stories we tell about our own life, the stories that constitute broadly the autobiographical self, help us manage the core self that registers minute-by-minute experience and imbues it with meaning. But do good stories—those exhibiting coherence, flexibility, and complexity—account for successful adaptation *or* reflect an ability to manage adversity?

The answer is: Both. Improving the quality of our self-understanding triggers new perspectives about situations, relationships, goals, and all the other decisive elements in a person's life. These new perspectives then influence how we respond. When we can reflect on our own responses, we become better at regulating our emotions, expressing ourselves more positively, and improving the environment in which we live.

Relative Recoveries

At all times of our lives, we want to make sense of the way people who matter to us treat us, to set their actions in a shared context, to read their moods, to understand how what they do and say is a response to what we do and say. In the absence of this basic coherence, the ground spins beneath us. We make hectic preparations for what we cannot understand or anticipate. We lead ourselves in a manic dance to adapt to a bizarre range of restrictions and responses, hoping that one day we will understand and manage our difficult environment. When we fail, we may be overcome by shame because we think we deserve the pain others may inflict on us. We may conclude that we are helpless and therefore give up any effort to improve our lives.

Recovery is relative. Resilience comes day by day, according to highly personal means and measures. The personal narratives we all engage in are ongoing acts of sense-making. These can be sources of renewal and growth. The healing powers come not from an expert who claims to hold the master key to interpretation, but from honing our skills to reflect, to understand, and to revise. Adults of any age can learn how to correct the vagueness and incoherence of their autobiographical stories, and can engage with others in ways that test and stretch understanding. The brain remains plastic—capable of learning and changing—throughout our lives. We may have to accept that, as

John Bowlby said, "One cannot ever really give back to a child the love and attention he needed and did not receive when he was small. With understanding and affection, and perhaps skilled help, one can go a long way toward it, sometimes a very long way, but it will never be quite the same."

However difficult our pasts, we cannot erase our histories. We need to remember and reflect to anchor our stories. The difficulty remains with us, but we can free ourselves from its power. For some people, remembering and clarifying their own stories is not enough. They may seek some way to repair a difficult relationship, believing that they can settle the terms of the dilemma once and for all. They may want to test whether they now have the skill to manage a relationship that once overwhelmed them. They ask: "Can I banish my fear and anxiety in my mother's presence? Can I now stand up to her? Can I speak honestly and openly now and not feel terror? Can I insist, 'This is who I am, and I won't cower even when I see that I displease you'?"

Day by day, you may catch yourself searching for mother love and maternal approval. You may decide to make a determined effort to relinquish the embedded hope that one day you'll get the long-sought response. You may decide to forgo the expectation that the difficult relationship will improve, either because your mother will change or because you will finally pull off the trick of pleasing her. The way forward may be to accept that, in her presence—either her physical presence or the internal model you retain—the dilemma will always be imposed, but you can decline to address its terms. Then your energies and focus can be directed toward obtaining pleasure, satisfaction, engagement, and resonance from other sources.

You may hear on a daily basis the punitive voice that you have internalized, the voice that casts suspicion and lodges accusations, or utters dire predictions and warnings. When you step back and record this shadow voice, you can see it for what it is: a remnant of past anxieties, a useless legacy. Peg Streep, pushing herself toward recovery, reflects: "Sometimes her voice echoes in my head in strange and unexpected ways, but it doesn't activate any triggers anymore. I can place the voice in the perspective of her life." The punitive voice inside your head can be tamed even if it is not fully silenced.

Sometimes we assess anew past criticism, condemnation, or retaliation and realize that our mother's approval is not worth what we have to give up in exchange. Sometimes we realize that our mother has changed, perhaps mellowed, perhaps put her own demons to rest. We gradually realize she is no longer so rigid or controlling or volatile, yet the internal arguments run on and on. To end the battle with her, we must win the battle with ourselves.

Recovery involves release from self-distrust; it is the ability to see through a fresh and flexible lens. It involves the ability to identify the varied responses and maneuvers that you used defensively against a difficult mother's dilemma; it replaces constraining defenses with more appropriate and creative coping strategies. Ultimately the challenge is not to resolve matters between you and your mother, but between you and the habitual, fear-based thought processes that come between you and your capacity to thrive on your own terms.

THERE IS ONE final piece of the puzzle about our experiences of a difficult mother and the possibility of recovery. You may have experienced your mother as difficult and be particularly sensitive to her moods, her displeasure, her criticism, or her lack of engagement because you carry a genetic vulnerability to difficult circumstances; but remember that the gene often referred to as the "depression-risk gene" is also called the "orchid gene" because of the delicacy associated with it. Some children are as hardy as dandelions, able to thrive in rough conditions; some children are vulnerable to difficult conditions. They may become depressed, or they may develop addiction or self-defeating dependence, or their anger may make them aggressive. This particular gene leaves you with a highly reactive amygdala (the fast-responding fear center of the brain) that makes you hypervigilant to others' responses; but it also gives you an edge across a wide range of learning. You are probably more attuned to people's responses and feelings. You are are probably quick to gauge the emotional temperature of language and gesture. What makes you vulnerable to a mother's flaws may also make you creative, reflective, and ultimately resilient.

The greatest release comes with the acceptance that it is not our mother who retains control over the fears, doubts, and dissatisfactions that we may have learned in the cauldron of our relationship with her. Release comes from relinquishing the urge to fight one more battle with her to gain recognition or acceptance or admiration. It is the enlightenment that our battle is no longer between ourselves and a mother but between the history that formed us and our better possible self.

Continuing the Emotional Audit

The claim made here is significant: Understanding why we find a mother difficult and how these experiences affect us can help us rewire our brains. We literally change our minds as we refine and reflect on our deepest emotions and embedded assumptions about ourselves and others. Old habits die hard, but the mind can remain active and plastic; in other words, we can always learn new ways of responding and adapting to challenges. Below are some questions to use to exercise resilience.

MAKE A LIST OF THE FEELINGS, ASSUMPTIONS, AND BEHAV-
IOR THAT YOU THINK RESULTED FROM YOUR EXPERIENCES
WITH A DIFFICULT MOTHER.

For each emotion, each assumption, and each habit on your list, focus on steps *you* can take to change them. Understanding—in the sense of seeing how difficult experiences with a mother gave rise to these self-defeating feelings, thoughts, and habits—is only the first step to resilience. The key question is: "How can you be effective in your own life?"

CONDUCT A HEALTH CHECK ON YOUR AUTOBIOGRAPHICAL SELF.

- List some typical interactions with your mother. Remember to test descriptions that contain, "She always . . ." and "She never . . ." Be on the lookout for expectations, because these universal statements about people and relationships are rarely accurate.
- Can you give specific examples to illustrate the general terms you use?
- Check whether there is a good fit between your general comments and the specific episodes and examples you provide.
- If there is a good fit, then your story is likely to be coherent, and you are at lower risk of reproducing your own difficult experiences.
- Test your ability to shift perspective. Can you see the

same events from different viewpoints? Check that what you write has a clear and consistent timeline.

- Try to notice your responses when someone else's behavior or your own feelings are confusing.

  Are you quick to blame others?

  Do you get angry?

  Do you launch into a tirade against yourself?

  Does being blamed for something send you into a spin of anxiety or anger?

- Identify what you are really anxious or angry about. Explain your feelings to yourself.

  Do you overreact to social awkwardness?

  Explain to yourself what result you fear from this awkwardness. Assess whether this fear or embarrassment is realistic.

- Do you still hope to resolve the difficult dilemma?

  Even though you may know on one level that you will never satisfy your mother, you find yourself hoping that one time you'll be what she wants you to be and that this will result in satisfaction and security. Think this through and consider whether it makes sense, given what you know. If it does not, then consider how you can move forward without getting that much-longed-for response from her. From what other sources can you receive recognition, understanding, and engagement?

- Before you continue your efforts to change the difficult relationship, ask yourself:

  Can you set aside the fantasy that all will be well between you and your mother if only you meet her expectations, needs, or standards?

Can you find some way of loving her without seeing yourself as a failure or disappointment?

Can you accept that your mother is not willing to get to know you? Or do you still feel crushing disappointment when she fails to listen responsively?

- Finally, focus on what you have learned from the difficulties in your relationship with your mother and the skills you have developed as you dealt with this relationship.

Can you see some positive aspects of your relationship with your mother?

Imagine how it feels to relinquish anger toward your mother.

Does this feel strange?

If so, try to identify the strangeness:

- Do you feel empty, as though you have given up an important part of your identity?
- Do you feel exposed, as though your anger has been protecting you from disappointment or the sudden shock of newly felt rage?

It may take time to identify different feelings:

- Try to separate your pain from resentment. While it is important to acknowledge the pain you have felt and understand its sources or the conditions in which it arose, it does not have to continue to shape your relationship.
- Try to look at familiar behavior through a new lens. At one time a mother's anger, control, narcissism, envy, or emotional absence struck deep within your psyche

because her responses were your mind's lifeblood. Now that you have your own routes to a coherent interpersonal world, her difficulties can shrink in significance, their power much reduced.

A difficult mother may present the dilemma: "Either meet my needs, expectations, and demands whatever the cost to yourself, or suffer coldness, condemnation, manipulation, or mockery." But you can gain the courage and power to say, "I find your coldness, condemnation, manipulation, or mockery unpleasant, but these will not change who I am nor will they destroy me. I can now see them for what they are. I will maintain a relationship with you, but I will not comply with the terms of the dilemma you try to impose."

It all seems obvious when we finally arrive at this position; but the route there is seldom easy. Nor is it visible from where we start. We ourselves have to attain the fresh vision that will put the endpoint in our sights. Each person has to find his or her own route, however many people struggle in similar ways before and after. No one can take this journey on our behalf; no one can spare us from it; but sharing common features of others' journeys may offer the guideposts we need.

Notes

A note on my use of pronouns: A child is sometimes referred to as "she" and sometimes as "he." The experiences I describe are common to both sons and daughters. Unfortunately, there is not a gender-neutral singular pronoun for "child." Hence, I sometimes use "they" when a singular pronoun is grammatically correct.

Introduction

viii **Difficult Mothers grew out of an article:** Apter, "Mother, Damned-est." This article was also carried in the UK by *The Independent*.

x **the term "good-enough mother":** Winnicott, *The Child, The Family, and the Outside World*, pp. 17, 44.

x **A good-enough mother is necessarily *not* a perfect mother:** Hopkins, "The Dangers and Deprivations of Too-Good Mothering."

x **"the client experiences her mother as difficult":** Josselson, *Playing Pygmalion*, p. xii.

xi **Other children have the genetic makeup of an orchid:** Dobbs, "The Science of Success." The specific gene is the mood-regulating gene known as the serotonin transporter gene or SERT. The shorter form of this gene is called the depression-risk gene. As well as being associated with a vulnerability to depression, it is associated with increased sensitivity to the emotional environment.

xiv **I refer to my own research:** See, for example, Apter, *The Confident Child*; Apter, *Altered Loves*; Apter, *You Don't Really Know Me*; Apter, *Secret Paths*.

xv **a thematic analysis of the transcripts:** Lieblich et al., *Narrative Research*; Josselson et al., *The Meaning of Others*.

Chapter One: *Difficult Mothers: Common Patterns*

5 **A good-enough mother has an ordinary person's:** Winnicott, "Primary Maternal Preoccupation."

10 **all unhappy families are pretty much alike:** Nabokov, *Ada*.

15 **learning how to integrate and regulate thoughts and emotions:** Schore, *Affect Regulation and the Origin of the Self*.

16 **"prolonged state of high arousal":** Rutter. "Today's Neuroscience, Tomorrow's History."

20 **This child may be highly reactive to fear:** Dobbs, "The Science of Success"; Bakermans-Kranenburg and Van IJzendoorn, "Parenting Matters."

Chapter Two: *The Science Behind a Mother's Power*

24 **A brain-stem reflex ensures:** Stechler and Latz, "Some Observations on Attention and Arousal."

24 **babies had no concept of what a person was:** Gopnik et al., *How Babies Think*, p. 26.

24 **the primary lessons of vital interpersonal relationships:** Cozolino, *The Neuroscience of Human Relationships*, p. 154.

24 **They stare longer at an image if it smells like their mother:** Acerra et al., "Modelling Aspects of Face Processing in Early Infancy."

24 **facilitates right-hemisphere to right-hemisphere communication:** Sieratzki and Woll, "Why Do Mothers Cradle Babies on

Their Left?" The theory about right-hemisphere to right-hemisphere communication has replaced the belief that mothers hold their babies on their left side (regardless of whether the mother herself is right- or left-handed) because the baby is soothed by the mother's beating heart. It has been noted that mothers who hold their baby on their right side may suffer from stress and possibly postpartum depression. Reissland et al., "Maternal Stress and Depression and the Lateralisation of Infant Cradling."

25 **they can recognize that a happy-looking face:** Gopnik et al., *How Babies Think.*

26 **simply obsessed by their baby:** Fleming and Corter, "Factors Influencing Maternal Responsiveness in Humans."

26 **new brain-imaging techniques show:** Cozolino, *The Neuroscience of Human Relationships,* p. 83; Seifritz et al., "Differential Sex-Independent Amygdala Response." Brains of fathers show similar activity under similar conditions.

26 **described as an elaborate flowing dance:** Stern, *The First Relationship,* p. 1.

27 **baby flirtation bypasses language:** Gopnik et al., *How Babies Think,* p. 31.

28 **the negative of that positive eye-to-eye engagement:** Josselson, *The Space Between Us,* p. 114.

31 **paradox has been described by the psychologist Carol Gilligan:** See, for example, Brown and Gilligan, *Meeting at the Crossroads.*

31 **"This is who I am":** Apter, *Altered Loves*; Apter, *You Don't Really Know Me.*

31 **apparent maturity forecloses self-exploration:** Erikson, *Childhood and Society.* Foreclosure is an unconscious decision to avoid the anxiety or complexity of the self exploration and role experimentation that teenagers normally engage in, and to opt instead for a simple, ready-made identity. A person who opts for foreclosure may be high-functioning and apparently confident, but is likely to be very limited in outlook.

33 **"Trying to understand human nature is part of human nature":** Gopnik et al., *How Babies Think,* p. 23.

34 **the crucial human skill called *mentalization*:** The concept of mentalization has been developed in a series of articles by Peter Fonagy. See Fonagy et al., "The Capacity for Understanding Mental States"; Fonagy, "Transgenerational Consistencies of Attachment."

34 **This complex response is called *marked mirroring*:** Fonagy et al., *Affect Regulation, Mentalization, and the Development of the Self.* The concept of marked mirroring is similar to Bion's notion of containment. See Bion, *Learning from Experience*; Fonagy, "Psychoanalysis Today."

35 **"The absence of attunement may be a non-event for a reptile":** Lewis et al., *A General Theory of Love*, p. 89.

35 **the ability to manage, control, and identify our own emotions:** Peter Fonagy calls this "affect regulation," or the ability to manage feelings. See Fonagy et al., *Affect Regulation, Mentalization, and the Development of the Self.*

35 **Learning how to regulate our emotional states:** Schore, "Attachment, Affect Regulation, and the Developing Right Brain."

36 **our early interpersonal environment creates a buffer:** Cozolino, *The Neuroscience of Human Relationships*, pp. 74, 221.

37 **the brain loses its remarkable plasticity:** Ibid., pp. 86–87.

39 **the implied messages that shape many parent/teen arguments:** Apter, *Altered Loves*; Apter, *You Don't Really Know Me.*

39 **Arguments with our mother:** Teenagers, both girls and boys, tend to have more interactions with a mother, and more arguments with their mother than their father. Montemayor and Hanson, "A Naturalistic View of Conflict Between Adolescents and Their Parents and Siblings"; Apter, *You Don't Really Know Me.*

40 **What damages a relationship:** Miller, *For Your Own Good.*

Chapter Three: *The Angry Mother*

47 **A classic example of the double bind:** The anthropologist Gregory Bateson introduced this concept, though it is now frequently associated with the psychoanalyst R. D. Laing. See Bateson, "Toward a Theory of Schizophrenia"; Laing, *A Divided Self.*

48 **Sometimes a difficult mother is defined as:** For example, see Streep, *Mean Mothers.*

53 **This state of terror is similar to:** Cozolino, *The Neuroscience of Human Relationships*, p. 257.

55 **a model for emotion and mood management:** Schore, *Affect Regulation and the Origin of the Self.*

55 **"rupture and repair":** Schore, *Affect Regulation and the Origin of the Self.*

55　**to build circuits and systems for emotional regulation:** Cozolino, *The Neuroscience of Human Relationships*, pp. 86–87.

56　**the more likely it is that anger will escalate:** Patterson and Forgatch, *Parents and Adolescents*.

56　**lurch again into an overwhelming sense of danger:** Cozolino, *The Neuroscience of Human Relationships*, p. 256.

58　**tool kit for managing their difficult environment:** Ibid., p. 232.

59　**Freud concluded that the game:** Freud, "Beyond the Pleasure Principle," pp. 7–64.

62　**"frozen image, or template":** Bank and Kahn, *The Sibling Bond*, p. 147.

63　**about to crash in on them or implode:** Laing, *A Divided Self*.

64　**no *conscious* memory of the event:** This provides an underlying explanation for post-traumatic stress disorder (PTSD). A common treatment for PTSD involves facilitating retrieval of the conscious memory so that the fear can be put in context and seen to have taken place in the past, in a specific context. The painful experience then becomes a specific event rather than a continuing trauma.

65　**"hold our mind in mind":** Allen et al., *Mentalizing in Clinical Practice*.

70　**you assume that strong feeling is tantamount to being out of control:** Cozolino, *The Neuroscience of Human Relationships*, p. 109.

71　**encourage others to treat you as your mother did:** Josselson, *The Space Between Us*, p. 16.

Chapter Four: *The Controlling Mother*

81　**preserves the "relationship" by exiting a real relationship:** Brown and Gilligan, *Meeting at the Crossroads*.

81　**Nancy Friday describes how her mother's refusal:** Friday, *My Mother, My Self*.

82　**"poisonous pedagogy":** Miller, *For Your Own Good*.

82　**Damasio likens this to a film:** Damasio, "Toward a Neurobiology of Emotion and Feeling."

85　**calls a "false self":** Winnicott, *The Maturational Processes and the Facilitating Environment*.

88　**In the name of love, they are accomplices:** Walker and Parmar, *Warrior Marks*.

89 **close down vital communication as they induct a daughter:** Gilligan, *The Birth of Pleasure.*

Chapter Five: *The Narcissistic Mother*

95 **a clinical diagnosis of "narcissistic personality disorder":** The *Diagnostic and Statistical Manual of Mental Disorders*, 4th edition, states that between 50 percent and 75 percent of those diagnosed with NPD are males. (American Psychiatric Association, *Diagnostic and Statistical Manual of Mental Disorders*, 4th edition. Washington, DC, APA 2000.) The forthcoming 5th edition (2013), however, has eliminated "narcissistic personality disorder" from the list on the grounds that it is less helpful to identify a prototype with the cluster of related traits than to make a general diagnosis of personality disorder with some specific narcissistic and manipulative traits. For a discussion see Zanor, "A Fate that Narcissists Will Hate."

96 **If you try to reason with her:** See the discussion of "narcissistic injury" in the *Diagnostic and Statistical Manual of Mental Disorders*, 4th edition, p. 715.

97 **Children who confront this dilemma:** Rappoport, "Co-Narcissism: How We Accommodate to Narcissistic Parents."

99 **experiences what is called "the collapse":** McBride, *Will I Ever Be Good Enough?*

Chapter Six: *The Envious Mother*

117 **paralyzing split between what has a false tone and what rings true:** See Bateson, "Toward a Theory of Schizophrenia"; Laing, *A Divided Self.*

117 **Melanie Klein described infantile love and rage:** Klein, *Envy and Gratitude and Other Works.*

118 **her easy delight in herself and her world infuriated her mother:** Streep, *Mean Mothers*, p. 1.

119 **Margaret Drabble depicts a mother:** Drabble, *The Peppered Moth.*

126 **generations of writers in the 1970s and 1980s:** See Eichenbaum and Orbach, *Between Women*; Chernin, *In My Mother's House.*

130 **pursuing the approval of others:** Kasser and Ryan, "Further Examining the American Dream."

Chapter Seven: *The Emotionally Unavailable Mother*

134 **as a child's concept of people became more sophisticated:** Feigelman, "The First Year."

135 **the child remains unresponsive:** Roberston, *A Two-Year-Old Goes to Hospital*; Bowlby, *Attachment*.

135 **and eventually detach from this bond:** See Bowlby, *Attachment*.

136 **Babies' rudimentary but finely tuned empathy:** The absence of these central human qualities—empathy, mind-reading and cooperation—can be seen in the devastating developmental deficiency called autism.

137 **a ghostly sense of "being there" and "being dead":** Green, "The Dead Mother."

140 **depression is mourning for a loss of one's self:** Freud, "Mourning and Melancholia."

142 **The running commentary . . . grinds to a halt:** There is some preliminary evidence that women who become mothers today are three times more likely to suffer from postpartum depression than were their mothers. Thirty years ago, 8 percent of new mothers suffered this illness; today, 27 percent of new mothers are diagnosed with postpartum depression, and a further 25 percent of new mothers report symptoms that indicate postpartum depression. Just when a child needs her mother's expressiveness and attunement most, the mother's levels of emotional energy are suppressed. See Gaynes et al., "Perinatal Depression."

142 **shows young children's rapid descent into despair:** Tronick and Cohn, "Infant-Mother Face-to-Face Interaction."

143 **less likely to have rewarding, compensating relationships:** Stein et al., "The Relationship Between Post-Natal Depression and Mother-Child Interaction."

143 **Affective sharing is an essential exercise:** Cozolino, *The Neuroscience of Human Relationships*, p. 221.

145 **he hopes to keep them both safe:** See Josselson, *The Space Between Us*, p. 30.

147 **they have foreclosed on their own opportunities for creative growth:** See Erikson on foreclosure, *Childhood and Society*.

147 **unable to grasp that other people saw the world differently:** Piaget, *Play, Dreams and Imitation in Childhood*.

150 **they have to be the dependable adult:** Erikson, *Childhood and Society*.

150 **his image of "mother" may be transformed:** Green, "The Dead Mother."

151 **children who share a mother may experience her very differently:** In one important study about the "separate lives" siblings experience even as they share a family, only one-third of the mothers in the study reported "a similar intensity and extent of affection" for both of their children, whereas two-thirds had some kind of preference, some sense that one child was a better fit, easier and more rewarding to engage with. Dunn and Plomin, *Separate Lives*, p. 64.

153 **does not register on his sluggish radar:** Moreover, the effect of postpartum depression on boys seems to be longer term and more severe than on girls, who may be better at eliciting responses they need from other caregivers. See Misri, *Shouldn't I Be Happy?* There is also evidence that a higher number of women suffer depression following the birth of a boy than the birth of a girl. See De Tychey et al., "Quality of Life, Postnatal Depression and Baby Gender."

158 **"Who would I be without my mother?":** Harrison, *The Mother Knot*, p. 45.

Chapter Eight: *Am I a Difficult Mother?*

164 **"I even feared that I might have to be done away with":** Roth, *Portnoy's Complaint*, p. 279.

164 **"Mother . . . is a sacred concept":** Streep, *Mean Mothers*, p. 6.

165 **"It is the suffering of ambivalence":** Rich, *Of Woman Born*.

165 **"One of the reasons it's hard to express satisfaction":** Roiphe, *Fruitful: A Real Mother in the Modern World*, p. 145.

165 **"I am talking in my Mr. Rogers voice":** Hanauer, ed., *The Bitch in the House*, p. 160.

166 **"These days, not only does it seem":** Ibid., p. 198.

167 **the good-enough mother's ability to reflect:** Hence, "reflection" in this context is a version of the process of "mentalization."

173 **Selma Fraiberg describes the ways:** Fraiberg, "Ghosts in the Nursery."

174 **"A thing which has not been understood inevitably":** Quoted in Bowlby, *A Secure Base*, p. 137.

175 **Yet it is difficult to map out new relational pathways:** Jacobvitz et al., "The Transmission of Mother-Child Boundary Disturbances Across Three Generations."

175 **Those who seemed ambivalent or detached:** Main and Solomon, "Procedures for Identifying Infants as Disorganized/Disoriented During the Ainsworth Strange Situation." Mary Main, who linked a parent's memory of her own childhood with her current behavior as a parent conducted this research. She categorized mothers in her study as "dismissing," "preoccupied," and "secure-autonomous," and in her analysis, their responses to questions about their childhoods were seen to correspond to attachment categories devised by Mary Ainsworth.

175 **evoked within a powerful "remembering context":** Karen, *Becoming Attached*.

175 **"This new remembering context":** Stern, *The Motherhood Constellation*, p. 181.

176 **levels of receptors for those stress chemicals:** Cozolino, *The Neuroscience of Human Relationships*, p. 112.

177 **children have evolved to be . . . "activists":** Hrdy, *Mother Nature*, p. 484.

177 **But as she uncovered the painful memories:** An important intervention involves coaching vulnerable mothers to respond actively to their children. This extends the learning process beyond uncovering negative memories to teaching skills of mother/baby interaction. See Fonagy et al., "The Capacity for Understanding Mental States"; Fonagy, "Transgenerational Consistencies of Attachment."

178 **protect her child from similar emotional harm:** Fraiberg, "Ghosts in the Nursery," p. 135.

179 **what could hurt and hinder their child:** Genevie and Margolies, *The Motherhood Report*, p. xxii.

185 **"Every life and childhood is filled with frustrations":** Miller, *For Your Own Good*, p. 254.

Chapter Nine: *Resilience*

187 what is called the "foundational relationship": Cozolino, *The Neuroscience of Human Relationships*, p. 114.

191 This process of engaging with others boosts: Gallagher, *I.D.: How Heredity and Experience Make You Who You Are*, p. 102.

192 that sick-making sensation of seeing ourselves: Stern, *The Motherhood Constellation*, p. 147.

193 The stories that form our autobiographical self: Damasio, "Toward a Neurobiology of Emotion and Feeling."

193 this seminal study led by Stuart Hauser: Hauser et al., *Out of the Woods*.

194 "Why did nine children become": Ibid.

199 "One cannot ever really give back": Quoted in Karen, *Becoming Attached*, pp. 110–11.

200 "Sometimes her voice echoes in my head": Streep, *Mean Mothers*, p. 135.

Bibliography

Acerra, F., Y. Burnod, and S. de Schonen. "Modelling Aspects of Face Processing in Early Infancy." *Developmental Science* 5 (2002): 98–117.

Adolphs, R. "Neural Systems for Recognizing Emotion." *Current Opinion in Neurobiology* 12 (2002): 169 77.

Ainsworth, M., M. Blehar, E. Walters, and S. Wall. *Patterns of Attachment: A Psychological Study of the Strange Situation.* Hillsdale, NJ: Erlbaum Associates, 1978.

Allen. J., P. Fonday, and A. Bateman. *Mentalizing in Clinical Practice.* Arlington, VA: American Psychiatric Publishing, 2008.

American Psychiatric Association. *Diagnostic and Statistical Manual of Mental Disorders,* 4th edition. Washington, DC: APA, 2000.

Apter, Terri. *Altered Loves: Mothers and Daughters During Adolescence.* New York: Fawcett, 1991.

———. *The Confident Child.* New York: W. W. Norton, 1997.

———. "Mother, Damned-est." *Psychology Today,* January/February, 2010: 80–87.

———. Secret Paths: Women in the New Midlife. New York: W. W. Norton, 1997.

———. You Don't Really Know Me: Why Mothers and Teenagers Daughters Fight. New York: W. W. Norton, 2004.

Bakermans-Kranenburg, M. J., and M. H. Van IJzendoorn. "Parenting Matters: Family Science in the Genomic Era." Family Science 1, no. 1 (2010): 26–36.

Bank, Stephen, and Michael Kahn. The Sibling Bond. New York: Basic Books, 1997.

Bartholomew, K., and L. Horowitz. "Attachment Styles Among Young Adults: A Test of a Four-Category Model." Journal of Personality and Social Psychology 61, no. 2 (1991): 226–44.

Bateson, G. "Toward a Theory of Schizophrenia." In Steps to an Ecology of Mind: Collected Essays in Anthropology, Psychiatry, Evolution, and Epistomology, Part III. San Francisco, CA: Chandler, 1972.

Bion, Wilfred R. Learning from Experience. London: Heinemann, 1962.

Bowlby, John. Attachment, 2nd edition. Attachment and Loss Series, Vol. 1. New York: Basic Books, 1983.

———. A Secure Base: Parent-Child Attachment and Healthy Human Development. New York: Basic Books, 1988.

Brandreth, G. "Was Enid Blyon the Mother from Hell?" Telegraph (UK), March 13, 2002.

Brown, Lynn Mikel, and Carol Gilligan. Meeting at the Crossroads: Women's Psychology and Girls' Development. Cambridge, MA: Harvard University Press, 1992.

Bruner, J. S. "Nature and Uses of Immaturity." American Psychologist 27 (1972): 1–23.

Byron, E., D. Jacobvitz, and L. A. Stroufe. "Breaking the Cycle of Abuse: Relationship Predictions." Child Development 59 (1998): 1080–81.

Cartwright, Duncan. Containing States of Mind: Exploring Bion's "Container Model" in Psychoanalytic Psychotherapy. London: Routledge, 2009.

Chernin, Kim. In My Mother's House. New York: Ticknor and Fields, 1983.

Cohen, L. B. 1979. "Our Developing Knowledge of Infant Perception and Cognition." American Psychologist 34 (1979): 894–99.

Cozolino, Louis. The Neuroscience of Human Relationships: Attachment and the Developing Social Brain. New York: W. W. Norton, 2006.

Crawford, Christina. Mommy Dearest. New York: William Morrow, 1978.

Crittenden, P. M. *Adult Attachment Interview: Coding Manual for the Dynamic-Maturational Method.* Milan, Italy: Cortina, 1999.

Damasio, A. R. "Toward a Neurobiology of Emotion and Feeling: Operational Concepts and Hypotheses." *The Neuroscientist* 1 (1995): 19–25.

Dennis, Patrick. *Auntie Mame: An Irreverent Escapade.* New York: Broadway, 2001.

De Tychey, C., et al. "Quality of Life, Postnatal Depression and Baby Gender." *Journal of Clinical Nursing* 17, no. 3 (February 2008): 312–22.

Deutsch, Helene. *The Psychology of Women: A Psychoanalytic Interpretation.* Boston: Allyn & Bacon, 1973.

Dobbs, David. "The Science of Success." *The Atlantic,* December 2009.

Drabble, Margaret. *The Peppered Moth.* New York: Harcourt, 2001.

Dunn, Judy, and Robert Plomin. *Separate Lives: Why Siblings Are So Different.* New York: Basic Books, 1990.

Eichenbaum, Luise, and Susie Orbach. *Between Women: Love, Envy, and Competition in Women's Friendships.* New York: Penguin, 1987.

Erikson, Erik. *Childhood and Society.* New York: W. W. Norton, 1964.

Estes, C. Pinkola. *Warming the Stone.* Boulder, CO: Sounds True CD, 1990.

Feigelman S. "The First Year." In R. M. Kliegman, , R. E. Behrman, H. B. Jenson, and B. F. Stanton, eds., *Nelson Textbook of Pediatrics.* 18th edition. Philadelphia, PA: Saunders Elsevier, 2007, chap. 8.

Fernald, A. "Four-Month-Old Infants Prefer to Listen to Motherese." *Infant Behavior and Development* 8 (1985): 181–95.

Fisher, Carrie. *Postcards from the Edge.* New York: Simon & Schuster, 2010.

Fivush, R. "Scripting Attachment: Generalized Event Representations and Internal Working Models." *Attachment & Human Development* 8, no. 3 (2006): 283–89.

Fivush, R., L. J. Berlin, J. M. Sales, J. Menniuti-Washburn, and J. Cassidy. "Functions of Parent-Child Reminiscing about Emotionally Negative Events." *Memory* 11, no. 2 (2003): 179–92.

Fleming, A. S., and C. Corter. "Factors Influencing Maternal Responsiveness in Humans. Usefulness of an Animal Model." *Psychoneuroendocrinology* 13 (1988): 189–212.

Folbre, N. *The Invisible Heart: Economics and Family Value.* New York: The New Press, 2001.

Fonagy, P. "Psychoanalysis Today." *World Psychiatry* 2, no. 2 (June 2003): 73–80.

———. "Transgenerational Consistencies of Attachment: A New Theory." Paper to the Developmental and Psychoanalytic Discussion Group, American Psychoanalytic Association Meeting, Washington, DC, May 13, 1999.

Fonagy, P., G. Gergely, E. Jurist, and M. Target. *Affect Regulation, Mentalization, and the Development of the Self.* New York: Other Press, 2002.

Fonagy, P., M. Steele, G. Moran, H. Steele, and A. Higgitt. "Measuring the Ghost in the Nursery: An Empirical Study of the Relation Between Parents' Mental Representations of Childhood Experience and Their Infants' Security of Attachment." *Journal of the American Psychoanalytic Association* 41 (1993): 957–89.

Fonagy, P., M. Steele, H. Steele, G. S. Moran, and A. C. Higgitt. "The Capacity for Understanding Mental States: The Reflective Self in Parent and Child and Its Significance for Security of Attachment." *Infant Mental Health Journal* 12 (1991): 201–18.

Fraiberg, Selma. "Ghosts in the Nursery: A Psychoanalytic Approach to the Problems of Impaired Infant-Mother Relationships." In F. Fraiberg, ed., *Selected Writings of Selma Fraiberg.* Columbus: Ohio State University Press, 1987, pp. 100–136.

Freud, Sigmund. "Beyond the Pleasure Principle." In *The Standard Edition of the Complete Psychological Works of Sigmund Freud,* vol. 18 (1920–1922). London: The Hogarth Press, 1955, pp. 7–64.

———. "Mourning and Melancholia." In *The Standard Edition of the Complete Psychological Works of Sigmund Freud,* vol. 14. London: The Hogarth Press, 1999, pp. 239–60.

Friday, Nancy. *My Mother, My Self.* New York: Delacorte Press, 1977.

Gallagher, Winifred. *I.D.: How Heredity and Experience Make You Who You Are.* New York: Random House, 1996.

Gardner, Howard. *The Mind's New Science: A History of the Cognitive Revolution.* New York: Basic Books, 1985.

Gaynes, B. N., N. Gavin, S. Meltzer-Brody, K. N. Lohr, T. Swinson, G. Gartlehner, S. Brody, and W. C. Miller. "Perinatal Depression: Prevalence, Screening Accuracy, and Screening Outcomes." Evidence Report / Technology Assessment, No. 119 (2005). Agency for Healthcare Research and Quality.

Geddes, H. "Attachment, Behavior and Learning: Implications for the Pupil, the Teacher and the Task." *Journal of Educational Therapy and Therapeutic Teaching* 8, no. 3: 231–42.

———. *Attachment in the Classroom: The Links Between Children's Early Experience, Emotional Well-Being and Performance in School.* London: Worth, 2006.

Genevie, Louis E., and E. Margolies. *The Motherhood Report: How Women Feel About Being Mothers.* New York: Macmillan, 1987.

George, C., N. Kaplan, and M. Main. *An Adult Attachment Interview: Interview Protocol.* Unpublished manuscript, University of California, Berkeley, 1985.

Gilligan, Carol. *The Birth of Pleasure.* New York: Alfred A. Knopf, 2002.

———. *In a Different Voice: Psychological Theory and Women's Development.* Cambridge, MA: Harvard University Press, 1982.

Gopnik, A., A. Meltzoff, and P. Kuhl. *How Babies Think: The Science of Childhood.* London: Weidenfeld and Nicholson, 1991.

Gottman, John. *Why Marriages Succeed or Fail.* New York: Simon & Schuster, 1995.

Green, Andre. "The Dead Mother." In Gregorio Kohon, ed., *The Dead Mother: The Work of Andre Green.* London: Routledge, 1999.

Hanauer, Cathi, ed. *The Bitch in the House: 26 Women Tell the Truth about Sex, Solitude, Work, Motherhood, and Marriage.* New York: Viking, 2003.

Hanzak, Elaine A. *Eyes Without Sparkle: A Journey Through Postnatal Illness.* Oxford, UK: Radcliffe Publishing, 2005.

Harrison, Kathryn. *The Mother Knot: A Memoir.* New York: Random House, 2005.

Hauser, Stuart T., Joseph P. Allen, and Eve Golden. *Out of the Woods: Tales of Resilient Teens.* Cambridge, MA: Harvard University Press, 2006.

Homberg, J. R., and K. P. Lesch. "Looking on the Bright Side of Serotonin Transporter Gene Variation." *Biological Psychiatry* (November 1, 2010).

Hopkins, Juliet. "The Dangers and Deprivations of Too-Good Mothering." *Journal of Child Psychotherapy* 22, no. 3 (1996): 407–22.

Hrdy, Sarah Blaffer. *Mother Nature: Maternal Instincts and How They Shape the Human Species.* New York: Ballantine, 2000.

Jacobvitz, D., et al. "The Transmission of Mother-Child Boundary Disturbances Across Three Generations." *Development and Psychopathology* 3 (1991): 517–25.

Josselson, Ruthellen. *Playing Pygmalion: How People Create One Another.* Lanham, MD: Jason Aronson, 2007.

———. *The Space Between Us: Exploring the Dimensions of Human Relationships.* San Francisco, CA: Jossey Bass, 1995.

Josselson, R., A. Lieblich, and D. P. McAdams, eds. *The Meaning of Others: Narrative Studies of Relationships*. Washington, DC: American Psychological Association, 2007.

Karen, Robert. *Becoming Attached: Unfolding the Mystery of the Infant-Mother Bond and Its Impact on Later Life*. New York: Warner Books, 1994.

Kasser, T., and R. M. Ryan. "Further Examining the American Dream: Differential Correlates of Intrinsic and Extrinsic Goals." *Journal of Personality and Social Psychology* 65 (1996): 410–22.

Klein, Melanie. *Envy and Gratitude and Other Works, 1946–1963*. New York: Delecorte, 1975.

Laing, R. D. *A Divided Self: An Existential Study in Sanity and Madness*. London: Penguin, 1965.

———. *Sanity, Madness and the Family: Families of Schizophrenics*. London: Penguin, 1990.

Lewis, Thomas, Fari Amini, and Richard Lannon. *A General Theory of Love*. New York: Vintage, 2000.

Lieblich, Amia, Rivka Tuval-Mashiach, and Tamar Zilber. *Narrative Research: Reading, Analysis, and Interpretation*. Thousand Oaks, CA: Sage, 1998.

Mahler, Margaret, Fred Pine, and Anni Bergman. *The Psychological Birth of the Human Infant: Symbiosis and Individuation*. New York: Basic Books, 1975.

Main, M. "Metacognitive Knowledge, Metacognitive Monitoring, and Singular (Coherent) Versus Multiple (Incoherent) Model of Attachment: Findings and Directions for Future Research." In *Attachment Across the Life Cycle*. C. M. Parkes, J. Stevenson-Hinde, and P. Marris, eds. London: Tavistock/Routledge, 1991, pp. 127–59.

Main, M., N. Kaplean, and J. Cassidy. "Security in Infancy, Childhood and Adulthood: A Move to the Level of Representation." *Monographs of the Society for Research in Child Development* 50, no. 1–2, "Growing Points of Attachment Theory and Research" (1985): 66–104.

Main, M., and J. Solomon. "Procedures for Identifying Infants as Disorganized/Disoriented During the Ainsworth Strange Situation." In *Attachment in the Preschool Years: Theory, Research and Intervention*, M. Greenberg, D. Cicchetti, and E. M. Cummings, eds. Chicago, IL: University of Chicago Press, 1990.

McBride, Karyl. *Will I Ever Be Good Enough? Healing the Daughters of Narcissistic Mothers*. New York: Free Press, 2008.

Meltzoff, A. N. "Infant Imitation After a 1-Week Delay: Long-Term Memory for Novel Acts and Multiple Stimuli." *Developmental Psychology* 24 (1988): 470–76.

———. "Foundations for Developing a Concept of Self: The Role of Imitation in Relating to Self and Others and the Value of Social Mirroring, Social Modelling, and Self Practice in Infancy." In *The Self in Transition: Infancy to Childhood*, D. Cicchetti and M. Beeghly, eds. Chicago: University of Chicago Press, 1990, pp. 139–62.

Meltzoff, A. N., and A. Gopnik. "The Role of Imitation in Understanding Persons and Developing a Theory of Mind." In *Understanding Other Minds: Perspectives from Autism*, S. Baron-Cohen, H. Tager-Flusberg, and D. J. Cohen, eds. New York: Oxford University Press, 1993, pp. 335–66.

Miller, Alice. *For Your Own Good: Hidden Cruelty in Child-Rearing and the Roots of Violence*. H. Hannun and H. Hannum, trans. London: Virago, 1987.

Misri, Shaila. *Shouldn't I Be Happy? Emotional Problems of Pregnant and Postpartum Women*. New York: Free Press, 2002.

Montemayor, Raymond, and Eric Hanson. "A Naturalistic View of Conflict Between Adolescents and Their Parents and Siblings." *Journal of Early Adolescence* 5, no. 1 (1988): 23–30.

Murray, L. "The Impact of Postnatal Depression on Infant Development." *Journal of Child Psychology and Psychiatry* 33, no. 3 (1992): 543–61.

Murray, Lynn, and Peter Cooper. *Postpartum Depression and Child Development*. New York: Guilford, 1997.

Murray, L., and C. Trevarthen. "Emotional Regulation of Interaction Between Two-Month-Olds and Their Mothers." In *Social Perception in Infants*, T. M. Fields and N. A. Fox, eds. Norwood, NJ: Ablex Publishing, 1985.

Nabokov, Vladimir. *Ada, or Ardor: A Family Chronicle*. New York: Vintage, 1990.

Nussbaum, Martha C. *Upheavals of Thought: The Intelligence of Emotions*. Cambridge, UK: Cambridge University Press, 2001.

Patterson, Gerald R., and Marion S. Forgatch. *Parents and Adolescents: Living Together, Part 1, The Basics*. Eugene, OR: Castalia Publishing Company, 1987.

Piaget, Jean. *Play, Dreams and Imitation in Childhood*. New York: W. W. Norton, 1962.

Pinter, Steven. *How the Mind Works*. New York: W. W. Norton, 1997.

Povinelli, D. J., and T. M. Preuss. "Theory of Mind: Evolutionary History of a Cognitive Specialization." *Trends in Neurosciences* 18 (1995): 418–24.

Rappoport, A. "Co-Narcissism: How We Accommodate to Narcissistic Parents." *The Therapist*, 2005. www.alanrappoport.com/pdf/ Co-Narcissism%20Article.pdf.

Rehm, Diane. *Finding My Voice*. New York: Alfred A. Knopf, 1999.

Reissland, N., B. Hopkins, P. Helms, and B. Williams. "Maternal Stress and Depression and the Lateralisation of Infant Cradling." *Journal of Child Psychology and Psychiatry* 50, no. 3 (2009): 263–69.

Rich, Adrienne. *Of Woman Born: Motherhood as Experience and Institution*. New York: W. W. Norton, 1976.

Roiphe, Anne. *Fruitful: A Real Mother in the Modern World*. Boston: Houghton Mifflin, 1996.

Robertson, James. *A Two-Year-Old Goes to Hospital*, A Scientific Film, 1952.

Roth, Philip. *Portnoy's Complaint: Novels 1967–1972*. New York: Library of America, 2005.

Ruddick, Sara. *Maternal Thinking: Toward a Politics of Peace*. New York: Ballantine, 1989.

———. "Care as Labour and Relationship." In *Norms and Values: Essays on the Works of Virginia Held*, J. G. Haber and M. S. Halfo, eds. Lanham, MD: Rowman and Littlefield, pp. 3–25.

Rutter, M. "Today's Neuroscience, Tomorrow's History. A Video Archive Project." Interview transcript. London: Wellcome Trust, 2008. http://www.ucl.ac.uk/histmed/downloads/hist_neuroscience_ transcripts/rutter.pdf.

———. "Continuities and Discontinuities from Infancy." In *Handbook of Infant Development*, J. Osofky, ed. New York: John Wiley & Sons, pp. 1256–96.

Sapphire. *Push: A Novel*. New York: Vintage, 1996.

Schore, Allan N. *Affect Dysregulation and Disorders of the Self*. New York: W. W. Norton, 2003.

———. *Affect Regulation and the Origin of the Self: The Neurobiology of Emotional Development*. Mahwah, NJ: Erlbaum, 1994.

———. "Attachment, Affect Regulation, and the Developing Right Brain: Linking Developmental Neuroscience to Pediatrics." *Pediatrics in Review* 26, no. 6 (2005): 204–17.

Seifritz, E., et al. "Differential Sex-Independent Amygdala Response to Infant Crying and Laughing in Parents Versus Nonparents." *Biological Psychiatry* 52 (2003): 1367–75.

Shafer, Roy. *Retelling a Life: Narration and Dialogue in Psychoanalysis.* New York: Basic Books, 1992.

Sieratzki, J. S., and B. Woll. "Why Do Mothers Cradle Babies on Their Left?" *Lancet* 347 (1996): 1746–48.

Stechler, G., and E. Latz. "Some Observations on Attention and Arousal in the Human Infant." *Journal of the American Academy of Child Psychiatry* 5 (1996): 517–25.

Stein, A., D. H. Gath, J. Bucher, A. Bond, A. Day, and P. J. Cooper. "The Relationship Between Post-Natal Depression and Mother-Child Interaction." *British Journal of Psychiatry* 158 (1991): 46–52.

Stern, Daniel. *The Birth of a Mother: How the Motherhood Experience Changes You Forever.* New York: Basic Books, 1998.

———. *The First Relationship: Infant and Mother.* Cambridge, MA: Harvard University Press, 1977.

———. *The Interpersonal World of the Infant: A View from Psychoanalysis and Developmental Psychology.* New York: Basic Books, 1985.

———. *The Motherhood Constellation: A Unified View of Parent-Infant Psychotherapy.* New York: Basic Books, 1995.

Streep. Peg. *Mean Mothers: Overcoming the Legacy of Hurt.* New York: William Morrow, 2009.

Trevarthen, C. "The Function of Emotions in Early Infant Communication and Development." In *New Perspectives in Early Communicative Development,* J. Nadel and L. Camioni, eds. London: Routledge, 1983, pp. 23–47.

Tronick, E. "Emotions and Emotional Communication in Infants." *American Psychologist* 44 (1989): 112–19.

Tronick, E., H. Als, L. Adamson, S. Wise, and T. B. Brazelton. "The Infant's Response to Entrapment Between Contradictory Messages in Face-to-Face Interaction." *Journal of the American Academy of Child Psychiatry* 7 (1978): 1–13.

Tronick, E., and J. F. Cohn. "Infant-Mother Face-to-Face Interaction: Age and Gender Differences in Coordination and the Occurrence of Miscoordination." *Child Development* 60, no. 1 (1989): 85–92.

Walker, Alice, and Pratibha Parmar. *Warrior Marks: Female Genital Mutilation and the Sexual Binding of Women.* New York: Mariner Books, 1996.

Walker-Andrews, A. S. "Infants' Perception of Expressive Behaviors: Differentiation of Multimodal Information." *Psychological Bulletin* 121 (1997): 437–56.

Warner, Judith. *Perfect Madness: Motherhood in the Age of Anxiety.* New York: Riverhead, 2005.

Watterman, Barbara. *The Birth of an Adoptive, Foster or Stepmother: Beyond Biological Mothering Attachments.* London: Jessica Kingsley, 2003.

Winnicott, Donald W. *The Child, the Family, and the Outside World.* London: Penguin, 1964.

———. *The Maturational Processes and the Facilitating Environment: Studies in the Theory of Emotional Development.* New York: International Universities Press, 1965.

———. *Playing and Reality.* London: Tavistock Publications, 1971.

———. "Primary Maternal Preoccupation." In *Through Paediatrics to Psycho-analysis.* New York: Basic Books; original edition published in 1956.

Zanor, C. "A Fate that Narcissists Will Hate: Being Ignored." *New York Times,* November 29, 2010.

Zeanah, C. H., and M. L. Barton. "Introduction: Internal Representations and Parent-Infant Relationships." *Infant Mental Health Journal* 10, no. 3 (1989): 135–41.

Acknowledgments

The idea for this book emerged from a piece I was asked to write for *Psychology Today*. As I gathered together my research and worked on the piece, I realized that this was a subject I had been grappling with for decades. It had remained in the periphery of my writing, a topic I tried to resist until the editors Carlin Flora and Hara Estroff Marano encouraged me to confront it. I am grateful to all those who contacted me about the article, explained what it had meant to them and pushed my work forward with their further questions. Yet some time remained before this subject shaped itself as a book. I was helped along the way by conversations and debates with colleagues, particularly Ruthellen Josselson and Janet Reibstein. Julia Newbery's enthusiasm for the research project she worked on at the Anna Freud Center on mothers and infants provided a key introduction to cutting edge findings on the role of mothers in brain development. Carol Gilligan's responses to the manuscript provided immeasurable help in refining the themes and variations of this highly sensitive topic. Susan Golombok expressed interest that helped sustain my own belief in the project.

From the beginning to the end of this project, my agent Meg Ruley provided crucial enthusiasm and support. My editor, Jill Bialosky, used her skills to detect a compact shape within the book's much looser drafts; her critical eye helped me focus, reminding me of my exceptional good fortune in having her as editor.

As always, the women and men who participated in my research are essential collaborators. They have been unstinting in their time and energy, and my debt to them is enormous.

Index

abandonment, 9, 11, 52–53, 115, 122, 125
  unconditional love vs., 48–49
abuse, 18–19, 78–79
  see also violence
acceptance, 21, 199–200, 201
  of blame, 44–45, 60–61, 66, 69, 102
accusation, via mindreading, 51
"acting out," 193, 196
acts vs. patterns, 3–4, 45–46, 64
addiction, 18, 51, 106, 107, 137–38, 144, 172, 201
adolescence see teenagers
affective sharing, 55, 143
  see also conversations, with infants
affect regulation, 210n
  see also emotional development; emotional intelligence
age, of children, view of mother affected by, xv, 1–2
Aikido approach, 171
Ainsworth, Mary, 215n
alcoholism, 18, 51, 137, 172
alloparenting, 136
ambivalence, maternal, 127, 141–42, 165–66

ambivalent attachment, 174, 215n
American Psychiatric Association, 212n
amour propre, 95
amygdala, 53–54, 64–65, 201, 209n
anger, 203
  of children at mothers, 105, 144, 201
  depression vs., 139
  escalation of, 56
  misplaced, 15, 50
  of narcissistic mothers, 96
  in normal families, 14–15, 45–46, 64, 161, 165, 166
  regulation of, 35
  relinquishing, 204
  unconscious, 165
angry mothers, xiii, 5–6, 14–16, 29–30, 43–73
  adult children of, 5–6, 29–30, 52, 62–73
  auditing effects of, 65–72
  barriers to challenging, 45–51
  blaming of child by, 47, 50, 169, 181–82
  coping mechanisms of children of, 15–16, 56–61
  developmental harm caused by, 15–16, 29–30, 53–61
  dilemma imposed by, 46–49

angry mothers (*continued*)
  fear of, 30, 48, 52–61
  internalization of voice of, 59, 61, 67, 71–72
  non-child targets of, 44
  perspective of, 43–44, 46–47
  physical experiences of, 56–58
  tactics of, 49–51
  unpredictability of, 6, 15, 29, 62, 72, 174
  violence of, 6, 15, 43, 52, 58, 66
Anna Karenina (Tolstoy), 9–10
anxiety, 4, 9, 15, 64, 176, 203
  as deflection, 170
  depression vs., 139
  regulation of, 35
  repetition compulsion and, 58–59
  separation, 134–36
  triggered by others' success, 111–12
  see also fear
anxious attachments, 174
Anywhere But Here (Simpson), 101–2
apathy, defensive, 134–35
appeasing, 11, 13
  of angry mothers, 59–60, 67–69
  of narcissistic mothers, 97–105, 108–10
approval, 115, 119, 120–21, 123, 130
Apter, Terri:
  methodology of, xiv–xv, 94
  as mother, 45, 76
  mother of, 7, 43–45, 75–76
  Psychology Today article by, viii, 227
Asperger's syndrome, 144
attachment:
  lost capacity for, 135
  patterns of, 174–75, 215n
attention, demands for, 146
attunement, 35–37
  see also mirroring
auditing *see* emotional audits
autism, 213n
autobiographical self, 82–84, 85, 131, 202–5
  see also stories

babies *see* infants
back talk, 79
"bad mothers," ix–x
Bateson, Gregory, 210n
"being there," 137
betrayal, 122, 144, 145
  by controlling mothers, 17, 75, 89
Bettleheim, Bruno, 190
Bion, Wilfred, 210n
birth order, 20, 151, 152–53

Bitch in the House, The (Hanauer, ed.), 165–66
blaming, 203
  of children, 47, 50, 119, 169, 181–82
  of self, in children, 44–45, 60–61, 66, 69, 102
bonding, 24–28, 174–75
Bowlby, John, 198–99
brain:
  amygdala of, 53–54, 64, 201, 209n
  of children, 37–42, 54–56
  cortisol receptors in, 143
  hippocampus of, 64–65
  of infants, 23–37, 54–55, 143
  limbic system of, 26, 53–54, 55
  memory and, 63–65
  of neglected infants, 36–37
  rewiring of, 178, 192–93, 198, 201
  right hemisphere of, 24–25, 54, 209n

caregivers, non-maternal, xii, 28, 38, 72, 133–36, 151, 191, 214n
case histories, xiv–xv
  Adam, 144–45, 152, 153
  Alandra, 145–46
  Amanda, 1
  Audrey, 62
  Bev, 103
  Camilla, 152–53
  Clara, 1
  Craig, 52, 86
  demographics of, xv
  Duncan, 138
  Eileen, 137–38, 140
  Elsa, 79–81
  Fay, 119
  Gabriel, 62
  Gary, 86
  Gina, 1
  Harriet, 103–4
  Jackson, 147–48, 156–57
  Jacqui, 105–6
  Jane, 137–38, 152
  Jenna, 7, 31
  Joel, 86
  Josie, 144–45, 152–53
  Kenny, 6–7, 30–31
  Kieran, 8, 32–33
  Komnan, 123
  Laura, 57–58, 60
  Lavinia, 79–80
  Lois, 46–47
  Magda, 1–2
  Margot, 46–47
  Pat, 99–100

Paul, 99–100
Paula, 87
Phil, 102
Rachel, 7, 32, 71
Robert, 52, 62
Sam, 57, 60
Sandra, 98–99
Sandy, 57, 60
Sarah, 2
Seth, 5–6, 29–30
Sonia, 8, 32–33
Steve, 62
Susie, 77
Tammy, 77
Tess, 120–21
change, 195
  see also flexibility
chaos, 14, 18, 21, 193
Chaucer, Geoffrey, 127
childcare, non-maternal, xii, 28, 38, 72, 133–36, 151, 191, 214n
childhood memories *see* memory
children:
  blaming of, 47, 50, 119, 169, 181–82
  as caregivers, 7, 18–19, 41, 144–48, 149–50, 152, 157
  as "difficult," 19–20
  empathy of, 147, 213n
  individual will of, 75–92
  normality as perceived by, 146, 149, 150–51
  options of *see* coping mechanisms; dilemmas
  responses to healthy anger by, 14–15
  self-blame in, 44–45, 60–61, 66, 69, 102
  sturdiness of, 135–36
  as subjective, x–xi, 3–4, 19–20, 44, 105, 131, 151
  unacknowledged suffering of, 49–50, 178–79, 184–85
  variety of responses among, xi, 19–20, 102–5, 151–53
  work done by, 146–47
  see also infants
combination tactics, 49–51
communication, 31, 188
  breakdown of, 12, 17, 189–90
  flawed, 167
  learning skills for, 26–29, 33–42, 163, 167, 178–79
  non-verbal, 176
  right-hemisphere, 24–25, 209n
  via mirroring, 30, 34–35, 37–40
  see also conversations

communities, xii, 28, 38, 72, 135–36, 151, 191, 214n
compartmentalizing, 31, 145–46, 191
competition, 88, 129
  with narcissistic mother, 96, 104, 107
conflict, patterns of, xi, 10, 11
confusion *see* unpredictability
"containers," 145, 158
containment, 210n
contempt, 170–71, 188
  from controlling mothers, 77, 78–80
  from envious mothers, 116, 121, 124
  from narcissistic mothers, 96, 97
context, 76, 102, 111
  remembering, 175–76, 177, 183
control:
  infantile fantasy of, 58–59, 117–18
  reasonable, 16, 76, 84, 162
controlling mothers, xiii, 6–7, 16–17, 30–31, 75–92
  auditing effects of, 90–92
  benefits from having, 92
  child's perspective on, 75, 79–80, 81, 86–87
  child's will broken by, 17, 76–77, 82
  in controlling cultures, 87–89
  dilemma imposed by, 86, 87–88, 89, 91
  enmeshment and, 84–87
  as experts, 75, 82
  inflexibility of, 16–17, 41, 76–77, 82, 90
  mirroring by, 30
  motivations of, 77–78, 85, 88, 89
  ordering by, 78, 79
  perspective of, 75, 80
  praise from, 6
  resistance to, 79, 80–81, 84
  saying "no" to, 6, 30
  sense of self damaged by, 78, 79–80, 83–87, 90–91, 189–90
  telling of child's story by, 82–84
  threatening by, 77, 78
  use of contempt by, 77, 78–80
  use of fear by, 77–78
conversations, 112
  anger used to end, 46, 47
  with infants, 26–28, 35, 55, 140, 142, 143, 163, 177, 183–84
  see also communication
coping mechanisms, 5, 8–9, 11–13, 15–16, 41–42, 58–61, 67–72, 138, 144–51, 191, 200
  acceptance, 44–45, 60–61, 66, 69, 102
  with angry mothers, 56–61, 67–72
  appeasing, 11, 59–60, 67–69, 191
  compartmentalizing, 31, 145–46, 191

coping mechanisms (*continued*)
damage limitation, 146–47
defensive apathy, 134–35
expecting the worst, 44
fixing things, 138, 139, 144, 147–48,
152, 155
getting perspective on, 67
hypersensitivity, 30
imitating, 144–45
internalizing, 59, 61, 67, 71–72, 90
lying, 80–81, 91
repetition compulsion, 58–59, 61
replication, 70–72
self-blaming, 44–45, 60–61, 66, 69, 102
stonewalling, 11, 15–16, 60, 69–70, 137
vs. interpersonal skills, 9, 35–36
core self, 82–84, 85, 125
see also self, sense of
counteraccusations, 50
criticism:
global, 169, 182
of mother, x–xi, 182–83
crying, 173, 177
culture, women constrained by, 87–89,
126–27, 133–36, 161–66
cycles:
breaking of, 162, 172, 175–79, 194
of control, 89, 92
Freud on, 174
generational, 2, 41, 45, 71–72, 162, 169,
171–80, 183, 215n
in other relationships, 68, 70–72, 92,
107, 109, 110, 172

damage limitation, 139, 146–47, 152
Damasio, Antonio, 82–83
"dandelion genes," xi, 20, 201
danger, 16, 37–38
see also fear
death:
desire for mother's, 1
of father, 86–87, 123
fear of mother's, 66, 157
fear of own, 28, 52, 66
mother's continued influence after, 20,
192
psychic, 137, 140, 141, 150–51
decision making, 90–92
defense mechanisms *see* coping mechanisms
defensive apathy, 134–35
denial, 170
of autobiographical self, 82
of children's feelings, 49–51, 167, 172,
190
of maternal envy, 116, 117, 120, 122,
126
dependence, 3, 4
of elderly mother, 192
memory and, 62–65
see also mothers, power of
depression, xiv, 130, 139–46, 201
coercion and, 148
genetic risk for, 201, 208n
grief and, 87
neglect and, 19
postpartum, 141–44, 153, 209n, 213n,
214n
see also emotionally unavailable mothers
Deutsch, Helene, 126
developmental psychology, xiii, 195
developmental stages *see* emotional development
*Diagnostic and Statistical Manual of Mental
Disorders* (APA), 212n
difference *see* gender; self, sense of
difficult mothers, xi, xii, 5, 8
auditing relationships with, 201–5
auditing risk of becoming, 179–85
barriers to insight by, 49, 166–71, 181–
83
benefits of having, viii, 21, 30, 68, 92,
109, 128, 157–58, 204
childhoods of, 41, 162, 169, 171–78,
179–80, 183, 215n
children of, as mothers, 2, 41, 45, 71–72
common patterns among, xiii, 1–21,
168–71, 174–75, 184–85, 188, 189,
190, 191
death of, 20, 192
difficulties of talking about, 1–2
difficulties of writing about, ix–xii
dilemma imposed by, 5, 8–9, 41, 174,
188–90, 191, 192, 199, 203, 205
as fluid category, 20, 39, 45, 86, 102, 122,
151–53, 176–77, 178–79, 200
identification of, xiv, 161–85
lifelong effects of, viii, 9, 17, 20–21, 33,
42, 73
love of, 47–49
numbers of, viii, xi, xv, 94, 174
objective views of, x–xi, 19–20, 44, 105,
130–31
overcoming, 187–205
protection against being, 166–68, 177–79
siblings' differing views of, 19–20, 102–5,
151–53, 214n
stages of response to, 13
vs. good-enough mother *see* good-
enough mother

see also angry mothers; controlling mothers; emotionally unavailable mothers; envious mothers; narcissistic mothers
"difficult relationships," xi
as two-way, 19–20, 102–5, 151–53
dilemmas, imposition of, 5, 8–9, 41, 174, 188–90, 191, 192, 199, 203, 205
  by angry mothers, 46–49
  by controlling mothers, 86, 87–88, 89, 91
  by emotionally unavailable mothers, 18–19, 138–39, 144, 148
  by envious mothers, 116–20, 123, 131
  by narcissistic mothers, 97, 107, 108, 111
discipline, healthy, 16, 193
disorganized attachments, 175
dissociation, 11, 15–16, 51
  from one's own feelings, 16, 47, 90–92, 148, 155, 188, 196
  see also stonewalling
distraction, normal, 133–36
double binds, 47–49, 116–18, 174, 210n
  see also dilemmas, imposition of
Drabble, Margaret, 119

emotional audits, xiv
  for all children, 201–5
  for mothers, 179–85
  of parental anger, 65–72
  of parental control, 90–92
  of parental emotional unavailability, 153–59
  of parental envy, 128–32
  of parental narcissism, 108–13
emotional development, 9, 23–42, 52–65, 101, 115, 117–18
  with angry mother, 48–49, 54
  neglect and, 36–37
  separation anxiety and, 134–37
  as social, 33–42, 143, 163, 187–88
  via eye contact, 24, 26–27, 28, 32–33, 135, 140, 173, 183, 184
  via fear, 25
  via mentalization, 33–37, 87
  via mirroring, 37–40, 54–55, 93–94, 96, 142–43, 183
  via questioning, 142
  via reflection, 49, 167
emotional intelligence, 167–68
  as acquired, 36, 142–43
  as basic need, 25, 33, 35–37, 40
  impairment of, 54–56, 142–43, 144, 146, 148–51, 196
  "orchid gene" and, 201

emotionally unavailable mothers, xiv, 8, 18–19, 32–33, 133–59
  adult children of, 138, 147–48, 153–59
  attempts to "fix," 138, 139, 144, 147–48, 152, 155
  auditing effects of, 153–59
  benefits of, 157–58
  compartmentalizing by children of, 145–46
  damage limitation with, 139, 146–47, 152
  as "dead," 137, 138, 150
  depression of, 19, 137, 139–46, 173
  dilemma imposed by, 18–19, 138–39, 144, 148
  harm to emotional intelligence by, 142–43, 144, 146, 148–51
  harm to sense of self by, 137, 142–43, 149, 151, 155, 158
  imitation of, 142–43, 144–45
  of infants, 8, 140, 142–43, 173, 177
  metaphors by children of, 137, 149, 150
  mirroring distorted by, 142–43, 145
  overcoming, 157, 158–59
  substance abuse by, 18, 137–38
emotional management, 54–56
emotions, 149
  complex, ix, xiii
  regulation of, 35–36, 54–55
  repression of, 188
  see also emotional development; emotional intelligence; *specific emotions*
empathy, 34, 147, 169, 213n
endogenous opiates, 24, 27, 38
enmeshment, 84–87, 121–24
envious mothers, xiv, 7, 17–18, 32, 115–32
  adolescence as trigger for, 122–23, 126–27
  auditing effect of, 128–32
  benefits of, 128
  challenging of, 130–32
  denial of, 116, 117, 120, 122, 126
  difficulty of leaving, 124–25
  dilemma imposed by, 116–20, 123, 131
  enmeshment and, 121–24
  gender bias of, 18, 119, 126–27
  harm to sense of self by, 121, 124, 125–26, 129–32
  motivations of, 118–19, 122, 126–28
  numbers of, 126–27
  perspective of, 116
  pleasure drained by, 7, 18, 117, 119, 123
  rebound effect from, 120–21
  recognizing, 116–17, 118, 121

envy, 116, 123, 127–28
exercises *see* emotional audits
explicit memory, 131–32
externalizing, 51
eye contact, with infants, 24, 26–27, 28,
    32–33, 135, 140, 173, 183, 184
"eye love," 26–27, 173, 184

false self, 85, 188
    see also self, sense of, damaging of
families, happy, 10, 115, 116, 118
    anger in, 14–15, 45–46, 64
    control in, 16, 76
    narcissism in, 100–101
    reflection in, 49, 166–68
    see also good-enough mother
families, unhappy, 10
fast-fear response, 53–55, 63–65, 70, 201
fathers, xii, 72, 209n
fear, 52–65
    of abandonment, 9, 11, 52–53, 115, 122,
        125
    for angry mother, 53
    of angry mothers, 7, 9, 30, 52–61
    in double binds, 48–49
    healthy, 25, 36, 55
    memory and, 63–65
    mirroring and, 38
    physiological response to, 53–54, 57–58,
        63–65, 70, 201
    regulation of, 35–36, 55, 58–61
    of success, 116–17, 123, 125–26, 129,
        132
    used by controlling mothers, 77–78
    see also anxiety
female circumcision, 88–89
Finding My Voice (Rehm), 61
first-stage response, 13
Fisher, Carrie, 107
flexibility, 12, 16–17, 38–40, 82, 90,
    167–68, 178–79, 195–96, 200
flight-or-fight response, 53–54, 63–65,
    70
flirting, with infants, 26–28
footbinding, 88, 89
foreclosure, 31, 145–46, 150, 209n
"foundational relationship," 187
    see also emotional development
Fraiberg, Selma, 173–74, 177–78
freedom, 76–77
Freud, Sigmund, 58–59, 174
Friday, Nancy, 81

gender, 20, 151
    envy and, 18, 119, 126–27

of interviewees, xv, 1–2, 3
    narcissism and, 95, 103, 212n
    of parents, xii
    postpartum depression and, 214n
    pronouns and, 207
    as subject to control, 88–89
generalized unhappiness, depression vs.,
    139
generational cycles, 2, 41, 45, 71–72, 162,
    169, 171–80, 183, 215n
genetics, resilience and, xi, 20, 152, 194,
    200–201, 208n
genital mutilation, 88–89
ghostly memories, 173–78
"Ghosts in the Nursery" (Fraiberg),
    173–74
Gilligan, Carol, 31
good-enough mothers, ix–x, 4–5, 8, 37
    complaints about, 3–5
    as difficult mothers to teens, 32, 39,
        122–23
    flexibility of, 12, 38–40, 76, 82, 90,
        167–68, 189
    judgments made by, 48–49
    vs. full-time mothers, 133–36, 162
    vs. perfect, x, 161–66
    see also families, happy; mothers
"good mothers," ix–x, xi, 133–36
Gopnik, Alison, 27, 33
grief, 86–87, 150
grudges, 96, 102
guilt, 124–26
    in children of depressives, 144–46, 158

Hauser, Stuart, 193–97
high-functioning facade, 147, 149–50,
    152, 209n
hippocampus, 64–65
"holding our mind in mind," 65, 92
Holocaust survivors, 176
hormones:
    of pleasure, 24, 27, 38, 53
    postpartum, 26, 27
    of stress, 143
Hrdy, Sarah Blaffer, 136, 177
hypersensitivity, 30

"identity reminders," 39, 189–90
imitation, 144–45
immaturity, length of human, 33, 136, 163
implicit memory, 131–32
implosion, 63, 111, 112–13, 165
imposter syndrome, 104–5, 109
incoherence, 11, 21, 49–50, 192
individuality *see* recognition; self, sense of

infants, 23–38
 care elicited by, 136, 163, 177, 178
 discomfort of, 34, 54
 emotion recognition by, 25, 136, 142–
  43, 213n
 eye contact with, 24, 26–27, 28, 32–33,
  135, 140, 173, 183, 184
 face recognition by, 24, 135, 183
 flirting with, 26–28
 instincts of, 24, 32–33, 135–36
 learning by, 25–26, 33–37, 142–43
 primitive envy of, 117–18
 rest needed by, 27, 184
 senses of, 24, 25, 55, 183–84
 separation anxiety in, 134–37
 as teachers, 177
 with unresponsive mothers, 8, 27–28,
  32–33, 140, 142–43, 173, 177, 215n
 see also emotional development
inner voice *see* internalization
insecure attachments, 174–75
insecurity *see* self, sense of
insight, 14, 21, 72–73, 91–92, 159, 166–
  68, 174, 178–80, 182, 185, 190–93,
  197–98, 201–5
 see also reflection
internalization, 61, 164, 192, 199–200
 of angry mother, 59, 61, 67, 71–72
 of controlling mother, 90
 of narcissistic mother, 98–99, 110, 113
interpersonal skills vs. coping mechanism,
  9

Jones, Claireece Precious (char.), 78–79
Josselson, Ruthellen, 10

Klein, Melanie, 117

Laing, Ronald D., 63, 210n
learning, 201
 as affected by childhood stress, 56
 by infants, 25–26, 33–37
 by mothers, 177–79, 183–84, 189, 215n
 from setbacks, 197, 198
Lewis, Thomas, 35
limbic system:
 of infants, 53–54, 55
 of mothers, 26
listening, 178–79, 189–90
 to avoid controlling, 82, 84, 87, 90
 lack of true, 170, 181, 184–85
 by psychologists, 195–96
love, 3, 5
 in double binds, 47–49, 50
 infantile, 117–18

introduced by mother, 24, 26–27, 28–29
 as a lie, 81
"low density narrators," 196
lying, 80–81, 91

MacLaine, Shirley, 107
magical thinking (reverse), 44–45
Main, Mary, 175, 215n
Mann, Doris (character), 107
marginalization, by angry mothers, 50
"marked mirroring" *see* mirroring
marriage, 100, 119, 139
masculinity, 89
"mask of motherhood," 141–42, 162,
  164–66
mastery, repetition compulsion and, 59
maternal ideal, ix–x, xi, 3, 48, 133–36,
  161–66
maturity, premature, 31, 147, 149–50, 152,
  209n
meaning, struggle for, 21, 33, 41–42, 167,
  187–89, 198
Mean Mother (Streep), 118
memory:
 controlled by mothers, 190
 effect of fear on, 63–65
 explicit vs. implicit, 131–32
 ghosts of, 173–78, 183
 questioning of, 181
 recovering of, 65, 173–74, 211n
 as therapeutic, 65, 174
 see also autobiographical self; stories
mentalization, 33–37, 87, 179, 184–85,
  214n
 see also insight; reflection
metaphors:
 by children, 6, 7, 47, 57, 62, 80, 105,
  119, 123, 137, 149, 150
 by mothers, 141, 162, 164, 165, 166
Miller, Alice, 82, 185
mind, understanding of *see* emotional
  intelligence; sense-making
mindreading, 51, 85, 107
"mini-mothers," 146, 152
mirroring, 30, 34–35, 37–40, 93–94, 183,
  210n
 as distorted by depression, 142–43, 145
 as distorted by envy, 119
 as distorted by narcissism, 94, 96, 119
 of teenagers, 38–40, 93–94
morality, teaching of, 14, 16, 44
mothers:
 ambivalence of, 127, 141–42, 161–65
 brain changes in, 26, 209n
 casual complaints about, 3–5

mothers (*continued*)
childhoods of, *see* cycles
children preferred unequally by, 214n
difficulty of renouncing, 9
flirting with infants by, 26–27
idealization of, ix–x, xi, 3, 48, 133–36,
161–66
infants' fantasies of, 58–59, 117–18
instincts of, 24–25, 26, 27, 90, 177, 184,
209n
in midlife, 126, 127
as model for intimacy, 23, 163, 167, 187
power of, 3, 12, 23–42, 93–94, 151, 162,
163–64, 205
role of, in emotional development,
23–42, 53–56, 142–43
seen as solely responsible for children's
well-being, xii, 133–36, 162
separation from, 58–59, 133–36
see also angry mothers; controlling mothers; difficult mothers; emotionally
unavailable mothers; envious mothers;
good-enough mothers; narcissistic
mothers
My Mother, Myself (Friday), 81

Nabokov, Vladimir, 10
narcissism, 94–96
healthy, 95, 100–101, 104
narcissistic mothers, xiii–xiv, 7, 17–18, 31,
41, 93–113, 169
adult children of, 98–100, 102, 103–4, 107
appeasing of, 97–105, 108–10
auditing effects of, 108–13
benefits of having, 109
child as proxy for, 97, 100–101, 103–4,
108, 111
dilemma imposed by, 97, 107, 108, 111
enabling of, 99–100
fragility of relationship with, 97–98, 108
harm to child's sense of self by, 98–99,
106, 109–10
imposter syndrome in children of,
104–5, 109
internalization of voice of, 98–99, 110,
113
mirroring distorted by, 93, 96, 119
number of, 94
rebellion against, 97, 105–7, 110
rejection by, 98, 102, 108
resolution with, 103, 107, 111–13
self-esteem of, 17, 95–97, 101, 103
"narcissistic personality disorder" (NPD),
95, 212n

Narcissus, 94
narratives, personal *see* stories
narrow vision, 50–51
nature, nurture and, 194
needs of child, subordination of, 5, 11, 31,
41, 149, 168–71, 178–79, 189–90
see also self, sense of, damaging of
neglect, 18–19
see also emotionally unavailable mothers
neuro-linguistic programming, 98
neuroscience, xiii, 23–42, 192–93, 209
fear and, 53–56, 64–65
infants and, 23–37, 54–55, 143
as route to recovery, 46
stress and, 15, 64–65
normality, children's perceptions of, 146,
149, 150–51
NPD (narcissistic personality disorder),
95, 212n
nurture, nature and, 194

obfuscation, 50
Of Woman Born (Rich), 165
operating assumptions, of children of
depressives, 149–51, 153–59
"orchid gene," xi, 12, 20, 194, 201, 208n
orphans, 134–35
"other," recognition of, 28, 187

pain, ratio of pleasure vs., xii, 5, 29
panic *see* fear
paradoxical feelings, ix, xiii
see also dilemmas, imposition of
parenting, normal *see* good-enough mother
Parmar, Pratibha, 88–89
"Parson's Tale, The" (Chaucer), 127
patterns:
of attachment, 174–75, 215n
of conflict, xi, 10, 11, 13
isolated acts vs., 3–4, 45–46, 64
Peppered Moth, The (Drabble), 119
"perfect mothers," ix–x
personality disorders, 95, 212n
personhood, xv
children's concept of, 118, 134
infants' concept of, 24, 134, 163
physical abuse *see* violence
placating *see* appeasing
play, 15, 58–59
pleasure:
effect of envious mothers on, 7, 18, 117,
119, 123
hormonal, 24, 27, 38, 53
ratio of pain vs., xii, 5, 29

"poisonous pedagogy," 82
  see also controlling mothers
Portnoy's Complaint (Roth), 164
Postcards from the Edge (film), 107
postpartum depression, 141–44, 153, 209n, 213n, 214n
post-traumatic stress disorder (PTSD), 211n
power, of mothers, 3, 12, 23–42, 93–94, 151, 162, 163–64, 205
praise, 6, 9
Precious (film), 78–79
projection, 102–3, 113
pronouns, 207
psychiatric hospitals, 193
psychic death, 137, 140, 141
psychological studies, 193–97
psychology:
  of fear, 52–61
  misinterpretations in, 135
Psychology of Women, The (Deutsch), 126
Psychology Today, viii
PTSD (post-traumatic stress disorder), 211n

race, xv
"real" mothers *see* good-enough mothers
rebellion, 97, 105–7, 110
rebound effect, 120–21
recognition, 38–40, 80, 85, 90, 93–94, 184–85
  enmeshment as barrier to, 121–22
  see also mirroring; self, sense of
reflection, 49, 166–68, 177, 179–80, 184–85, 192–93, 194, 199, 214n
  see also insight
regret, 118–19, 127, 128
Rehm, Diane, 61
rejection, 47–49
  by narcissistic mothers, 98, 102, 108
relationships:
  continuity of, 134, 136–37
  difficult, xi, xii
  fragile, 97–98, 108
  mother as model for, 23, 163, 167, 187–88
  negotiating of, 38–40
  pain-to-pleasure ratio in, xii, 5, 29
  repairing, 199
  replicating of *see* cycles
  shell vs. real, 31, 80–81
  sustaining, 195, 197
  as threat to mother, 99–100
"remembering contexts," 175–76, 177, 183
repetition compulsion, 58–59, 61

replicators, 70–72
  see also cycles
resentment *see* envious mothers
resilience, viii, xiv, 187–205
  development of, 55, 91–92, 158–59, 201
  genetics and, xi, 20, 152, 194, 200–201, 208n
  as not about changing mother, 199–200, 201, 203–5
  stories for developing, 187–88, 190–200, 202–3
resistance, rebellion vs., 106
responsiveness, x, 90
Reynolds, Debbie, 107
Rich, Adrienne, 164–65
right hemisphere, 54
  communication via, 24–25, 209n
Roiphe, Anne, 165
Roth, Philip, 164
rules *see* control
"rupture and repair," 55

sadness, depression vs., 140
Schappell, Elissa, 166
"schema," 63
second-stage response, 13
secure attachments, 174
self, autobiographical, 82–84, 85, 131, 202–5
  see also stories
self, sense of, 12, 17, 23–29, 33–36, 37–40, 54–55, 82–83, 85, 93–94, 95, 115, 163, 187–88, 195–98
  core, 82–84, 85, 125
  of depressives, 140, 145
  false, 85, 188
  of narcissistic mothers, 17–18, 169
  shifting of, 158–59, 197–98
self, sense of, damaging of, xii, xvi, 11–13, 16–17, 27–33, 36–37, 38–39, 41–42, 168–71, 178–79, 187–90
  by angry mothers, 49–51
  by controlling mothers, 78, 79–80, 83–87, 90–91, 189–90
  by emotionally unavailable mothers, 137, 142–43, 149, 151, 155, 158
  by envious mothers, 121–23, 124, 125–26, 129–32
  by narcissistic mothers, 98–99, 106, 109–10
self-blaming, 44–45, 60–61, 66, 69, 102
self-control, 55, 76
self-defeating behavior, 105–7, 109–10, 129–30, 193, 201

self-punishment *see* internalization
self-soothing, 35–36, 58–61
sense-making, 21, 33, 41–42, 167, 187–89, 198
senses, of infants, 24, 25, 55, 183–84
separation anxiety, 133–36
serotonin transporter gene (SERT) *see* "orchid gene"
sexual activity, 79, 80, 81, 89
shame, 16, 61, 68, 69, 106, 110, 120
shell relationships, 31, 80–81
siblings, 19–20, 102–5, 151–53, 214*n*
    as "mini-mothers," 146, 152
    rivalry between, 166
silence, as harmful, 176
Simpson, Mona, 101–2
"Snow White," 126
social beings, humans as, 33–34, 41–42, 167, 198
spankings, 43
    see also violence
Stern, Daniel, 175–76
stimulus-response conditioning, 131
stonewalling, 60, 69–70
    see also dissociation
stories, 193–98
    closed, 167, 168
    controlled by mother, 83–84, 85, 181, 188, 190–91
    inconsistent, 171–72, 180, 202
    of self, 82–84, 92, 112, 159, 179–80, 187, 202–5
    teen study of, 193–97
    see also memory
Streep, Meryl, 107
Streep, Peg, 118, 164, 200
stress:
    emotional management effected by, 55–56, 58–61
    genetic tolerances for, xi, 12, 20, 194, 201, 208*n*
    regulation of, 15, 31, 36–37, 54–55
substance abuse, 18, 51, 106, 107, 137–38, 144, 172, 201
success:
    fear of, 116–17, 123, 125–26, 129
    of others, 111–12
success of child:
    as justification for control, 88
    on mother's terms, 97, 102, 104–5, 107
    as trigger *see* envious mothers
suffering, unacknowledged, 49–50

suicide attempts, 106, 125, 144, 148
survival, 28
    of Holocaust, 176
    as social, 33–34, 41–42, 167

tactics, of difficult mothers, 49–51, 124–26, 168–71, 184–85, 188
teenagers, 38–40, 91, 93–94, 97–98, 101
    demands of, 31, 39, 93–94
    envy aroused by, 122–23, 126–27
    independence of, 1–2, 3, 31, 38–40, 78, 190
    institutionalized, 193–97
    rebellion suppressed by, 31, 145–46, 150, 209*n*
    tensions between parents and, 1–2, 3, 31, 77–81, 84, 93–94, 210*n*
therapy, 72, 87, 195
third-stage response, 13
Tolstoy, Leo, 9–10
trauma, 63–64, 176, 211*n*
    see also violence
trust, 118
    lack of, 150–51
"trying to improve the script," 59–60
    see also appeasing

unconditional love, 48–49
unconscious memories, 64, 173–74, 175–76, 183, 211*n*
understanding *see* insight
unhappiness, depression vs., 139
unpredictability, 6–7, 10, 14, 15, 97

Vale, Suzanne (character), 107
van Ogtrop, Kristin, 165, 166
violence:
    of angry mothers, 6, 15, 52, 61, 63–64, 66, 169, 190
    children's fantasies of, 58
    cycles of, 41, 70–72, 172
    emotional, 36, 58
    see also abuse
"Visit from the Footbinder, A" (Prager), 88
vulnerability, xi, 20, 41–42, 53

Walker, Alice, 88–89
Warrior Marks (Walker), 88–89
Winnicott, Donald, 85
witness consciousness, 65, 67, 92, 113
work/home balance, 133–36, 162
writing, as therapeutic, 67, 113, 131–32